# The Owner's Manual

## A Man's Guide to Health and Vitality through the Lens of Car Maintenance

**Ron Green, DC**

**The Owner's Manual**



Website: theownersmanual.life

ISBN: 978-1-0688972-2-1

# Contents

# Introduction

"Knowledge isn't power until it is applied."

—Dale Carnegie

Your body is a moving machine, not unlike an automobile. It is built to last about one hundred years, and we get away with a lot up until about forty years of age, at which point the aging clock kicks in and bad lifestyle habits-e.g., overeating, physical inactivity, and lack of sleep-start to take their toll. Similarly, after about 100,000 miles, a car will start to show the effects of wear and tear.

We all know that cars require regular maintenance to function optimally, including oil changes, tire rotations, and tune-ups. By the same token, men need to undergo routine screenings and make good lifestyle choices to stay in top physical condition. Sometimes you have to pay a visit to the clinic to deal with a sprain or ache, just as a car needs to go to the shop to have a dent worked out or a malfunction corrected. (The benefit of being human, however, is that the body is generally self-healing.)

# Introduction

Inspired by the owner's manual of a car, this manual is yours to use as a guide, reference, and reminder to get on and stay on the path of good health. Habit change is difficult, but by being persistent and learning what works best for your body, you can turn yourself into a finely tuned machine. By knowing how to maintain your human machine each day and over the years, you may steer clear of experiencing breakdowns, unnecessary pain and suffering, and all their associated costs.

If you follow the advice contained in this book, which even includes a Basic Maintenance Schedule at the end of Part 3, you may avoid many of the health problems that seem to affect so many men at one point or another in life or catch a problem early enough to "repair" it, so to speak. This manual is meant to shift your mindset from treatment to prevention. Nevertheless, always consult with your healthcare practitioner before engaging in any strenuous exercise or diet change, or if any "warning lights" turn on, such as pain, dizziness, fatigue during the day, sudden weight loss, or night sweats. Ignoring the troublesome signs coming from your car or your body can lead to more significant issues down the road.

Part One
# Before You Start

# Basic Models—Body Types

"Every body type can achieve health and fitness; it's about finding the right approach and staying consistent."

—Lou Schuler

When it comes to cars, there are a few basic car models out there on the road. When it comes to human beings, the same concept applies. In general, there are three body types, and one of these types is you! The terms *endomorph, mesomorph,* and *ectomorph* are commonly used to describe these body types, which are defined by factors such as bone structure, muscle mass, and fat distribution. (See Figure 1.1. Body Types below.) Each body type generally comes in small, medium, and large sizes.

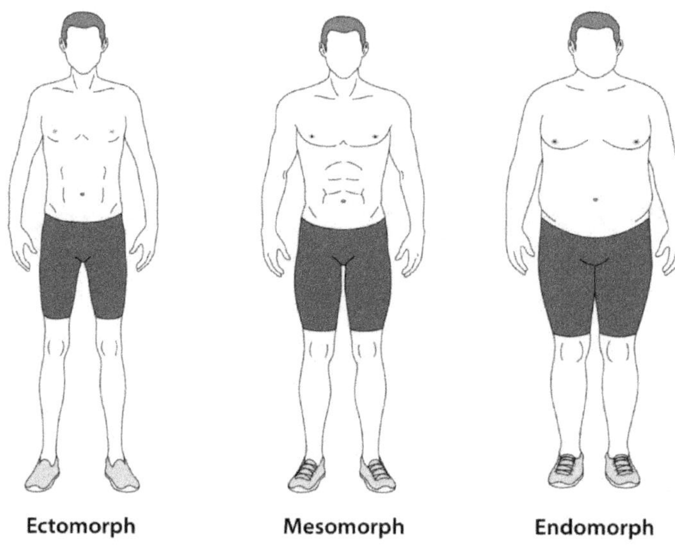



*Figure 1.1. Body Types*

## ECTOMORPHS

Ectomorphs are typically characterized by a lean and slender build, with narrow shoulders and hips. They tend to have a fast metabolism, giving them a naturally slim and lightweight physique and making it hard for them to put on muscle and fat. The ectomorph is the hybrid sedan of body types, thanks to its efficiency, lightness, sleek design, and agility.

## MESOMORPHS

Mesomorphs are naturally muscular with a balanced bone structure. They tend to put on muscle and fat more easily than ectomorphs. The mesomorph is the crossover vehicle of body types, having a rugged build while also being nimble and streamlined. Much like how a crossover vehicle delivers high performance and deftness even in difficult conditions, mesomorphs possess a strength and swiftness that allows them to display their athleticism with ease, which also helps them to stay fit.

## ENDOMORPHS

Endomorphs tend to have a softer, rounder physique than both ecto-morphs and mesomorphs, with a higher percentage of body fat and a bigger bone structure. Like mesomorphs, they tend to put on muscle and fat easily. The endomorph is the SUV or truck of body types, beefy and tough. If you were putting together a football or rugby team, you would likely want to fill your front line with endomorphs.

## NOTE

Whichever body type you happen to have, it is important to know that any one of them can be transformed into a toned, powerful specimen. Any car can become a muscle car, so to speak. And although older models may need more warming up, they can still look and perform great on the highway.

# Alignment—Posture

"A good stance and posture reflect a proper state of mind."

—Plato

Car alignment is similar to posture, in that it is related to maintaining balance, stability, and overall efficiency and performance. Just as proper car alignment ensures that a vehicle will remain steady on the road, good posture promises stability for a human being. Misaligned wheels can cause a vehicle to pull to one side, causing tires to wear unevenly, which can lead to volatility and potentially dangerous driving conditions. When it comes to humans, misalignment can lead to pain and weakness.

Good posture allows for efficient movement and reduces strain on muscles and joints. Maintaining good posture enhances comfort by reducing stress on the body, just as proper car alignment contributes to a smoother ride by reducing vibrations and uneven tire wear, enhancing overall driving comfort.

Correct car alignment is essential for safety on the road, as it supports predictable handling and responsiveness, reducing the risk of accidents. Likewise, correct posture—both static and dynamic—is a crucial component of injury avoidance. When a neutral posture is maintained (i.e., when you maintain the correct amount of curvature in the neck, mid back, and low back), your back will be able to handle the stress of gravity on the spinal structures, including the discs, ligaments, and muscles. Back problems most often stem from either a chronic static position like sitting at a desk with poor posture (head forward and back hunched) or from acute injury, such as might occur from lifting an object while having a flexed low back. Essentially, introducing new stressors, such as shearing or rotational stress, on the spinal structures puts these structures at risk, increasing the chance of back injury.

Just as a car requires a solid and stable chassis to deal with bumps in the road, you need your spinal structures to be strong so you can manage life's hurdles in stride, and maintaining good posture is the best way to ensure their strength. Neglecting car alignment can result in costly repairs and possible safety hazards over time. Poor posture can lead to chronic health issues such as back pain, muscle strain, instability and early degenerative changes. Correct skeletal frame alignment dictates that the shoulders, hips, knees, and ankles be aligned and sit directly on top of each other. All vertical and horizontal planes should be straight and level. If all the joints are aligned, then the head sits balanced and relaxed on top of the shoulders. (See Figure 1.2. Deluxe Model below.)

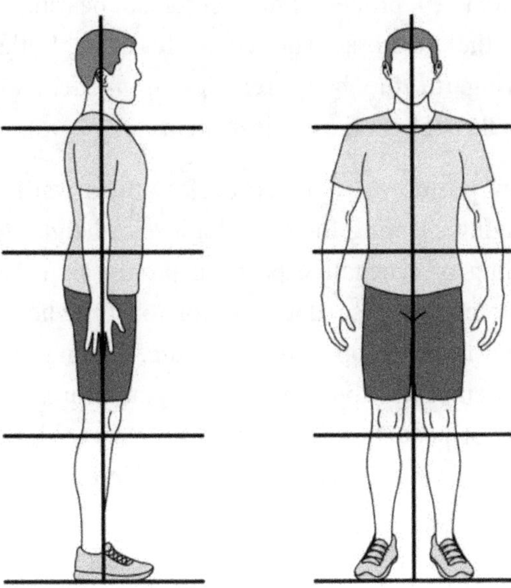

*Figure 1.2. Deluxe Model*

The spine and pelvis must be strong if they are to support the weight of the body. The shoulders and hips are ball and socket joints that should be highly mobile and sturdy in order to propel the body efficiently. The spinal discs, knee menisci, and soft tissue (especially muscle) are like the primary shocks and suspension system. We are designed to deal well with compression loads, but problems arise from consistently poor posture. When your head, which weighs approximately ten pounds, sits atop your shoulders in a balanced manner through good posture, you incur a reasonable compression load. If your head starts to go forward, however, you then introduce a shearing force along with this compression force, causing your posterior neck muscles to work very hard to hold your head up. The effects on your discs, joints, ligaments, and muscles become equivalent to what you would experience if your head were to weigh twenty pounds. Basically, poor posture leads to structural breakdown.

When the spine is in proper alignment, load bearing is distributed evenly among the vertebrae and centrally through the discs. The nerves, or wiring, of the body remain unimpeded, allowing fluid communication throughout the entire system.

The modern-day posture of slumped back with forward head carriage results in damaging shearing forces and a loss of height over time. It is just the beginning of a negative postural progression that accelerates degeneration. Joint and disc degeneration occur when muscles and ligaments can no longer support the structure, leading to a remodeling of bone in an attempt to support this failing structure. In other words, having this type of posture will cause your bones to distort over time. (See Figure 1.3. Effects of Poor Posture Over Time.)

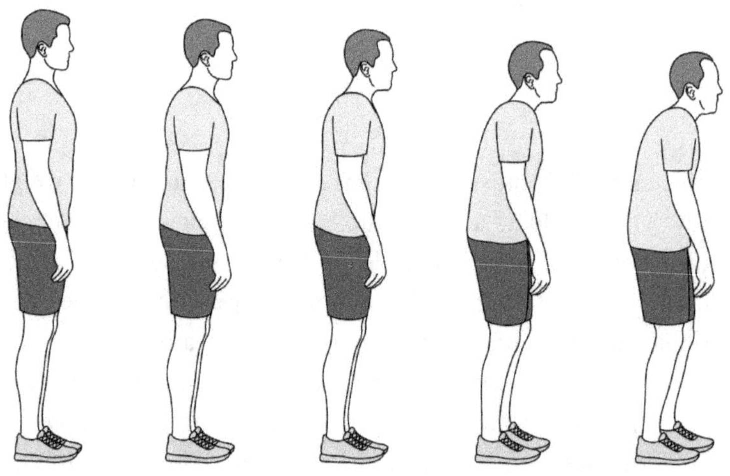

*Figure 1.3. Effects of Poor Posture Over Time*

## TIPS

Be aware of your posture. Strive to maintain a neutral spine most of the time, demonstrating normal amounts of spinal curvature, with your head balanced on top of your shoulders. Pay attention to any signs of discomfort or pain in your spine. Ignoring such symptoms can lead to more significant issues. (Consult a healthcare professional if you experience persistent or severe back pain.) And stay hydrated, as water is essential for maintaining the elasticity and fluidity of the spinal discs. Drink plenty of water throughout the day to keep your discs and other tissues hydrated and healthy. The following tips are meant to promote good posture in everyday activities.

**Workstation Ergonomics**

The science of ergonomics concerns designing objects that allow an individual to maintain a neutral body position and perform actions in a manner that minimizes stress on the body, thus decreasing the likelihood of incurring an injury over time from repetitive low-grade stressors. Try to adjust your workspace to reduce strain on your spine. If you work on a computer, use an ergonomic chair and desk, and position your monitor appropriately to support good posture. Whether you are sitting or standing, your eyes should be looking somewhere between the middle and the top of your monitor's screen, your elbows should be bent at a 90-degree angle, and your wrists should be in a neutral position. When using a laptop for long periods, elevate it to eye level by using a stand or stacked books and attach a separate mouse and keyboard. If you have a sit-and-stand workstation, alternate between these two work positions throughout your day. (See Figure 1.4. Workstation Ergonomics below.)

If you stand at your workstation, consider standing on a Topo Mat, which is a mat with lumps and ridges that offer your feet alternative positions and support, helping to prevent your feet from becoming tired. If you work on two screens or more, remember to swivel your chair when changing your screen gaze. Do not twist your head or body when looking at the other screen and set up all screens at the proper eye level.

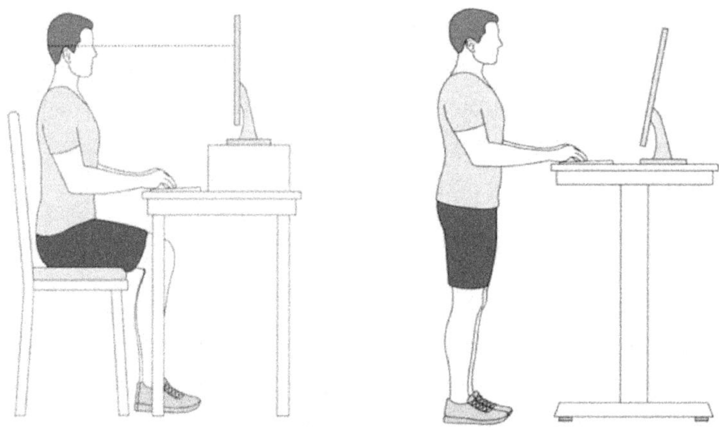

*Figure 1.4. Workstation Ergonomics*

If you sit at your desk, take a break from your workstation every 30 to 40 minutes by going for a short walk or, if time does not permit, simply stand up for a few seconds and sit right back down. Don't get stuck on completing a task all in one sitting. Use a movement reminder, such as an app that tells you to move after a specific period of time. Remember that we are built for movement, not stagnation.

## Sitting

Do not collapse into a low-energy slouching posture. If you feel yourself starting to slouch, get up and move around to re-engage your deep spinal muscles. If you must cross your legs, cross them at the ankle instead of the knee, or at least alternate crossing with your other leg to avoid uneven pelvic muscle length.

## Driving

To get in and out of your car, sit down on your buttocks first and then swivel your legs in or out. Sit in an upright position, relax your shoulders, and grip the steering wheel at the nine and three o'clock positions, most of the time. Ensure that all mirrors are set up properly, and that you do not find it difficult to check your blind spot. In addition, try not to rest your arm on the windowsill or center console for long periods of time.

## Standing

Try not to stand with more weight on one leg for too long. Instead, subtly shift your weight from one leg to the other, like doing a slow dance, or rock back and forth from your heels to your toes. If you work in a standing position, remember to take breaks and move around, just as you would when sitting, as the stabilizing muscles of the spine and pelvis "turn off" when you get stuck in the same position over a long period of time. In other words, if you would like these muscles to do their job well, they regularly need to be activated by moving.

## Wearing a Backpack or Single-Strap Bag

Be sure to wear your backpack evenly on both shoulders and utilize the waist strap to handle most of the load. For a single-strap bag or purse, if possible, carry it cross-body style, not all on one side of the body. When walking longer distances, alternate shoulders. (See Figure 1.5. Wearing a Backpack or Single-Strap Bag below.)

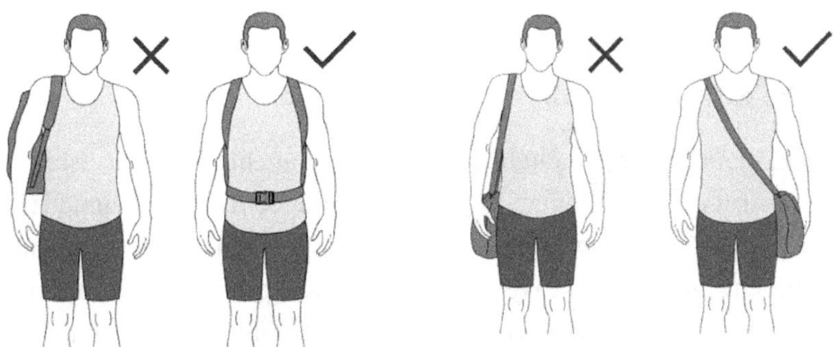

*Figure 1.5. Wearing a Backpack or Single-Strap Bag*

## Sleeping

You should awaken well rested and without pain every morning. To get out of bed, lie on your side and let your feet and legs fall off the side of the bed first, and then raise the rest of your body into a sitting position. If your mattress is more than ten years old, consider getting a new one. When testing a new mattress, be sure to spend more than ten minutes lying on it to see if it maintains support of your spine. Try a few different pillows to see what works best to support your head. Either sleep on your side and use an extra pillow between your knees, or sleep on your back with an extra pillow under your knees. Avoid sleeping in twisted positions. (See the Battery Recharge section in Part 2 for information on pre-sleep preparation.)

## Lifting

When lifting an object, use proper lifting technique by bending your legs while keeping a straight and stiff back and your abdominal muscles engaged. Use your leg muscles by bending at the knees, hinging at the hips and keeping your spine in a neutral position. Keep the object close to your body and avoid twisting while lifting it. When moving the load, do not twist your back, instead, shuffle your feet into position while maintaining a neutral spine.

## MAINTENANCE GUIDE

Regular maintenance, including periodic alignment checks, is essential for preserving a car's longevity and performance. Likewise, practicing good posture and incorporating ergonomic principles into your daily routine can help you to avoid posture-related problems and promote your long-term musculoskeletal health. (See Figure 1.6. Unbalanced vs. Balanced Vertical Posture below.)

To maintain good posture, make a point to perform posture exercises throughout the day. These exercises can be done anywhere, should be done every day, like brushing and flossing your teeth, and may be performed in a sitting or standing position. They will train your muscles in such a way as to bring you into good posture and keep you there. What's more, most of them can be accomplished as you are waiting in a line, walking, or working at your workstation.

For each exercise, hold the position for 10 to 30 seconds, or perform 10 repetitions (reps) of the exercise one to three times a day.

**Vertical Posture Strategies**

There are a number of simple strategies to help bring your head to balance on top of your shoulders, which include:

- visualizing stacking and balancing your vertebrae on top of each other, and then consciously relaxing your muscles.
- pretending to zip up your sweater or jacket to the top.
- pulling or tucking in your chin.
- pretending someone is pulling the hair on the crown of your head, upward.

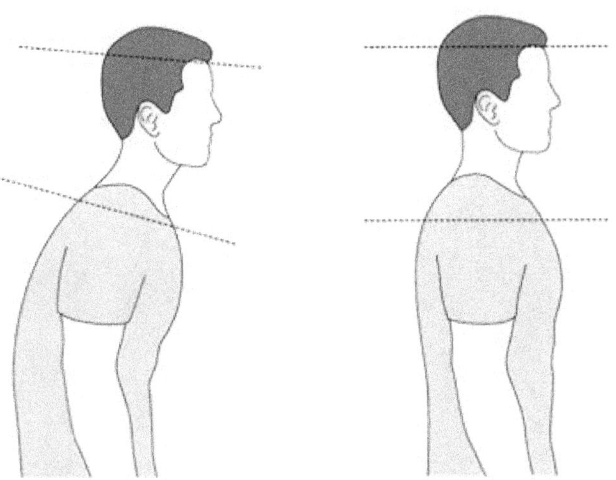

*Figure 1.6. Unbalanced vs. Balanced Vertical Posture*

## Door Stretch

Stand in front of an open doorway and place your arms and hands on either side of your door frame. (See Figure 1.7. Door Stretch below.) Gently step through the doorway and feel the stretch at the front of your chest. These muscles often shorten due to a person's hunched over posture, so it is important to stretch and lengthen them out so that it is easier to maintain an upright posture. Hold this position without letting your head tilt forward for about 10 seconds. Repeat as needed.

*Figure 1.7. Door Stretch*

## Vacation Pose

Interlace your fingers at the crown of your head and look to the horizon. (See Figure 1.8. Vacation Pose below.) Relax your shoulders and hold this pose for 10 seconds.

This exercise stretches the shoulders and strengthens the upper back and neck, helping to keep you from slumping forward.

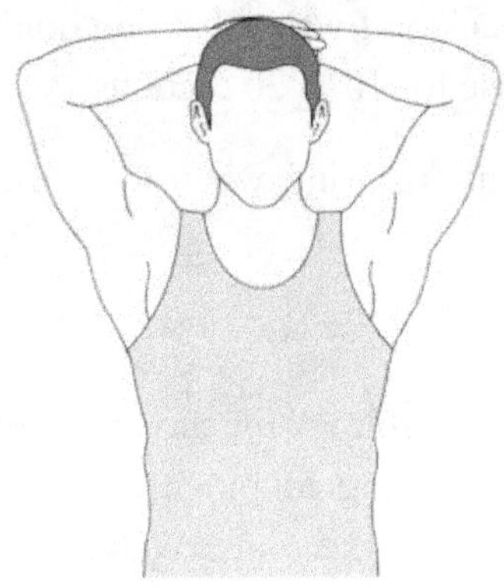

*Figure 1.8. Vacation Pose*

## Short Foot

Grip the floor with your foot and drag your forefoot in, essentially doing a pull-up with the arches of your foot. (See Figure 1.9. Short Foot below.) Perform this exercise 10 times for each foot or hold the end position for 10 seconds. Strong and stable feet muscles are better able to help support the entire body weight.

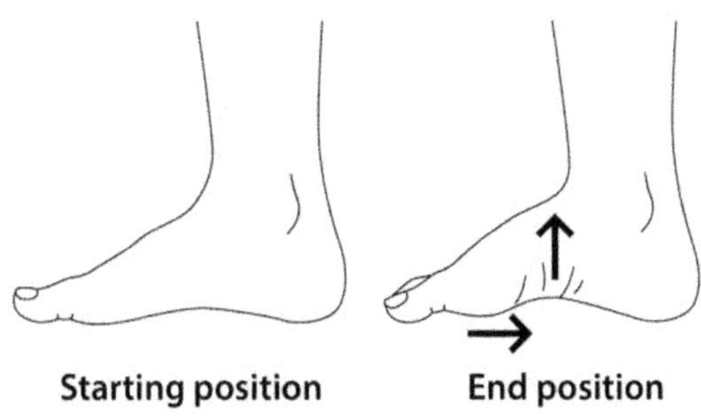


*Figure 1.9. Short Foot*

**Abdominal Stiffening**

This exercise may be performed in any position. Tighten or stiffen your abs and attain a level pelvis, both front to back and side to side. Think of your pelvis like a bucket of water that you don't want to spill in any direction. Hold this pose for 10 to 20 seconds.

Abdominal strength and knowing when to use them is necessary for injury prevention.

**Butt Clench**

This exercise may be performed in any position. Clench your butt cheeks together by pretending to pinch a dollar bill between them. Hold this pose for 10 to 20 seconds. Walking up stairs and vertical inclines such as hills can also develop these muscles.

Butt muscles are often weak and need to be strong to balance out often tight quads.

**Quad Stretch**

Quadricep (quad) muscles often become shortened due to prolonged sitting. This stretch can be performed in a standing position or while lying on your side. Gently hold on to your ankle, foot, or pant-leg cuff of one leg (if you are not flexible enough) and gently pull it in the direction of your buttocks until you feel a stretching sensation at the front of your thigh. (See Figure 1.10. Quad Stretch below.) When performing this exercise, it is important to maintain a level pelvis and head. Do not pull your heel to your buttock too hard as it may compromise your knee. Hold this pose for 10 to 20 seconds.

*Figure 1.10. Quad Stretch*

## NOTE

If you don't feel aligned properly, make an appointment with a good chiropractor (i.e. an alignment specialist), who will help to re-establish the proper mobility of your joints. If your joints are too tight, the chiropractor will use adjustive techniques to adjust the tension/torque of the joint to normal levels. If there is too little torque on certain joints and they are too loose, then a chiropractor, physiotherapist, physical therapist, occupational therapist, or personal trainer can teach you specific exercises you can use to tighten them up. In either case, an underlying issue may need to be addressed, such as inflammation or scar tissue, in order to stabilize the joint.

## CAUTION

As you may already know, cell phone usage is a posture destroyer. Use with caution.

# Tires—Footwear

"Good shoes take you to good places."

—Seo Min Hyun

Like tires on a car, shoes are often the interface between your foot (and everything above it) and the ground. Shoes provide you with traction, stability, and protection, just as tires do for a car. And, of course, both shoes and tires undergo wear and tear over time due to usage and exposure to various conditions.

Both tires and shoes can experience uneven wear patterns. Tire misalignment, improper inflation, or suspension issues can cause uneven tire wear, leading to decreased performance and potential safety concerns. In shoes, uneven wear may result from walking or running gait abnormalities, or from wearing shoes that don't fit properly. Completely worn-out tires compromise vehicle handling, braking, and overall safety on the road. Worn-out shoes can cause discomfort and increase the risk of foot-related injury. Regular maintenance is necessary to ensure optimal performance and safety.

## MAINTENANCE GUIDE

Regular maintenance is required to prolong the lifespan of both tires and shoes. For tires, maintenance includes proper inflation, rotation, alignment, and periodic inspection for damage or irregular wear. For shoes, it may involve cleaning, conditioning, and replacing worn-out soles and heels.

But footwear maintenance isn't just about the shoes; it's also about the feet. Strengthening your feet improves the overall grip and stability of your footwear, just as inflating tires supports proper traction and balance. Foot-strengthening exercises include doing ankle circles in each direction and the short-foot exercises described earlier.

When showering, be sure to wash your feet and between your toes, and wear flip flops or water shoes when using a public shower or walking around a public pool area to prevent toe fungus. Clip your toenails and remove toe jam regularly to prevent toenail problems such as ingrown toenails, thickened and discolored nails due to fungal infections, toenail trauma from nails catching on objects, and difficulty walking or wearing shoes comfortably due to overly long nails. Finally, purchase quality socks; you deserve them!

Despite regular maintenance, however, your shoes are still going to need replacement at some point.

## REPLACEMENT

Ignoring the signs of wear and continuing to use tattered shoes can lead to diminished performance, safety risks, and potentially painful outcomes, just as driving on threadbare tires can lead to costly repairs or accidents. When purchasing a new pair of shoes, look for the following qualities:

- **Good flexion control.** The shoe should bend where the forefoot meets the base of the toes.
- **Firm heel counter.** The shoe should have a sturdy heel counter to support and connect your heel-to-shoe complex. A heel

counter is a structure built into the back of a shoe to support the wearer's heel and its proper connection to the shoe so that the foot does not move around inappropriately inside the shoe.

- **Stiffness in torsion.** The shoe should be difficult to twist out of shape.
- **Proper heel height.** The height of the shoe's heel should be no higher than 1.5 inches, otherwise you'll feel as though you're walking downhill.
- **Comfort.** The shoe should be comfortable from the moment you try them on.
- **Wide enough toe box.** The shoe should not be so tapered at the toe that it squishes your toes together. Set your toes and forefoot free!

Shop for shoes in the afternoon or evening, as your foot naturally expands with use during the day, and purchase shoes made by respected manufacturer (e.g., Asics, Brooks, Saucony etc.). When shopping for footwear, seek out a knowledgeable salesperson who will not rush you, and be sure to try on many pairs, comparing their levels of support and comfort. Walk around the store when testing shoes. Try a different shoe on each foot and notice the difference. Pay attention to width as well as length. If you use orthotics, bring them so you can try them with neutral-fit shoes.

If you don't use orthotics, you may be wondering what they are. Orthotics are shoe inserts that control uneven damaging forces by creating proper alignment and shock absorption. By correcting foot and ankle alignment, ground forces are properly distributed up through the knees, hips, pelvis, and low back.

You may benefit from orthotics if any of the following statements apply to you:

- When examining your shoes, you notice unequal wear.
- Your feet flatten and your ankles collapse inward when you stand.

- You have foot or heel pain.
- You have loose ligaments from a previous ankle injury.
- You stand most of the day, especially on hard surfaces.

Finally, if you have foot and lower body problems that persist regardless of your having good shoes, you may need orthotics, which may be custom made or bought off the shelf, depending on your specialist's recommendations.

**NOTE**

Older folks may want to consider wearing a barefoot, or minimal, shoe for increased sole-to-ground awareness, which may prevent falls. This type of shoe *has a very thin sole,* which enables the wearer's feet to feel the ground better.

If you find yourself dealing with callouses, foot or toe fungus, corns, or other foot problems often, you may wish to see a foot professional, otherwise known as a chiropodist or podiatrist.

# Part Two

# "Driving"

# Locomotion—Movement

"We do not stop exercising because we grow old. We grow old because we stop exercising."

—Dr. Kenneth Cooper

The minimum amount a car should be driven is at least once every week to prevent maintenance issues such as the battery losing its charge and tires developing flat spots if the car sits for too long. Further, a lack of use can allow for developing rusted brakes and dried out seals. By driven, we mean for at least 10 miles, including some highway speeds to help keep it running smoothly. Humans similarly benefit from movement, in that it helps to keep the joints lubricated and flexible—not allowing "rust" to take hold, so to speak—and to maintain muscle strength and joint stability. Furthermore, the swinging motion you make with your arms and legs when you move (especially when walking) helps to push your lymph fluid through your lymph node filters, cleaning it. It is for this reason that your lymph nodes are concentrated in the groin and arm pit areas of your body. In addition, the muscle contractions that occur during movement move your blood and lymph fluid throughout your system, ensuring adequate oxygen supply and waste removal, respectively. Movement is a required activity, every day!

## MAINTENANCE GUIDE

Daily movement should include at least 4,000 steps a day, taken at a medium pace. To strengthen your bigger muscles, be sure not to skip the stairs or inclines along the way. You may want to use an activity tracker or pedometer to monitor your daily movement and keep yourself on track. Another way to approach it would be to keep moving throughout the day if possible, taking small breaks for no longer than 20 minutes at a time. If you are injured or have mobility issues, you may supplement your limited walking with biking or using a stationary bike, swimming, elliptical machine, or rowing machine.

## TAKE A MOVEMENT BREAK

If you are sedentary for extended periods of time, you can always reestablish normal muscle length, lubricate your joints, and activate the intrinsic stabilizing muscles around your spine and pelvis by taking a two-minute "movement break" every 20 minutes or so.

Examples of full body movements include:

- going for a walk while swinging your arms freely.
- dancing.
- using a rebounder.
- performing arm-swing squats, which involve making a movement similar to the one you might have done as a child when you would jump up to grip the monkey bars. Simply don't include the jump! (See Figure 2.1. Arm-Swing Squat below.)

*Figure 2.1. Arm-Swing Squat*

## TIPS

When in motion, walk with your head level and use your eyes to look down, not your head. Take the stairs over short escalator or elevator trips. Park a little farther from your destination. Get into the daily habit of taking a break from your smartphone by turning it off between specific times of the day. Don't stay idle for more than 20 minutes, and remember to stand, sit, and move with good posture.

# Engine—Muscles

"People who exercise regularly can gain up to three hours of life for each hour of exercise."

—Harvard Alumni Study

Maintaining muscle mass is akin to maintaining your car's engine. Just as regular check-ups keep your car's engine humming and ensure a smooth, reliable ride, exercising the muscles helps you to have the strength and stability needed to support your structure and pump life giving blood efficiently throughout your body.

In both cars and people, investment in regular maintenance, whether it's routine servicing for a car or exercise for a person, pays off in sustained performance, reduced risk of breakdowns, and overall longevity. Neglecting car maintenance will surely lead to the deterioration and failure of the vehicle, while ignoring your muscular fitness will eventually result in your physical decline and increased vulnerability to health problems.

Routine engine tuning and occasional upgrades allow a car to handle increased demands, such as higher speeds or heavier loads. Regular exercise allows your muscles to adapt to increased demand, enhancing your ability to handle various physical tasks and stresses. Strong muscles will improve your physical performance, energy levels, endurance, and support efficient metabolism. Properly maintained cars perform better, consume fuel more efficiently, and have longer lifespans. Well-conditioned muscles do the same thing.

Regular engine servicing prevents major breakdowns, costly repairs, and extends the car's lifespan just like regular exercise prevents injury, age-related muscle loss (i.e., *sarcopenia*) and metabolic disorders.

## ANY MODEL CAN BE A MUSCLE CAR

A muscle car is like a finely tuned athlete. Its engine roars with the vitality of a sprinter bursting from the starting line. This car isn't just about raw power; it's about balance, precision, and endurance.

When you exercise, you build and strengthen your muscles, tendons, and bones. Exercise fortifies your skeletal muscles, which support your frame and organs, and bolsters your heart muscle (perhaps the most important bodily "engine") to drive your body steadily. You also improve your cardiopulmonary and cardiorespiratory systems and promote robust nerve functioning and hormonal activation. Exercise builds skeletal muscle, which acts as joint padding and boosts shock absorption in your joints. It also creates a muscle reserve, which can be beneficial if you get sick. Therefore, it is crucial  that you make exercise a priority, especially as you age!

It will take up to six weeks of consistent exercise to reach a base level of fitness that you can build upon. Once you attain this base level of fitness, you can add variety and intensity to your exercise regimen for growth and shaping or sculpting exercises for aesthetics. You can also add a fun factor by exercising to music, joining a class, or trying different types of workouts and equipment. For exercise to be a consistent lifestyle habit, it must be accessible, attainable, time effective, and, of course, do no harm.  For exercise to be especially effective, you must try hard,

## Caution

Avoid injury at all costs as injury will set you back and prevent or hinder forward progress. Find a good trainer to work with to teach you good technique and set you up with a safe exercise program.

# Gears—Heart-Rate Zones

"Action is the fundamental key to success."

—Pablo Picasso

Like the gears of a car, heart-rate zones refer to levels of intensity. Each heart-rate zone has a different effect on our physiology. Heart-rate zones are defined as a percentage of one's maximum heart rate (HR max) attained through intense physical exertion and include:

- Heart-Rate Zone 1: Low (50% to 60% HR max)
- Heart-Rate Zone 2: Low to medium (60% to 70% HR max)
- Heart-Rate Zone 3: Medium (70% to 80% HR max)
- Heart-Rate Zone 4: Medium to high (80% to 90% HR max)
- Heart-Rate Zone 5: High (90% to 100% HR max)

Knowing which heart-rate zone you are in can maximize the effectiveness and safety of your workout.

## MAINTENANCE GUIDE

The goals of a basic fitness program include maintaining the heart and skeletal muscles strength and endurance along with skeletal muscle flexibility. Exercise can be done safely and effectively by including a good warm-up and a gradual buildup of intensity over time, and by picking the best exercises for yourself so that you can enjoy their benefits without having to face frustration and down time due to injury. If you are unfamiliar with exercising, then it is a good idea to get some help from a certified personal trainer.

### Warming Up

Just as you should warm up your car before driving on a cold morning, warming up your body will prepare it for the demanding activity of a workout by lubricating joints and bringing more blood to the muscles. A warm-up is meant to prime your body for activity. Be sure to warm up your body for at least 5 to 10 minutes before engaging in strenuous exercise. This can consist of brisk walking or jogging, or the use of an elliptical machine or stationary bike at low intensity, followed by light full-body movement. Finally, make sure you are well hydrated before engaging in activity.

### Cardio

Fitness requires efficient air intake to oxygenate the blood, as well as a good heart and blood vessels to distribute this life-giving blood to all parts of the body. Effective cardio exercise includes low-intensity steady-state (LISS) cardio and high-intensity interval training (HIIT) cardio. It is important to determine which type of exercise will be effective, sustainable, and non-injurious for you to do when you push the proverbial pedal to the metal. Low intensity steady state cardio is scientifically recommended to perform two to three times a week. This level of exercise should be done within heart-rate zones 2 or 3, so you should just be able to carry on a conversation while in this zone.

If possible, get your LISS exercise outdoors, walking, hiking, running, swimming, cycling, paddling, or rowing. You may also do your LISS cardio indoors on a treadmill, elliptical machine, stationary bike, rowing machine, or stair climber, or in an indoor swimming pool.

High-intensity interval training involves repeated bouts of high-intensity effort followed by brief recovery times. This type of exercise should be performed within heart-rate zone 5 for 10 to 15 minutes, two to three times a week. There are numerous benefits to HIIT, including burning a lot of calories. There are many options for HIIT's work-to-rest ratio. You may choose to exercise at high intensity for 30 seconds followed by a rest period of 15 seconds (2:1 ratio), or for 30 seconds followed by a rest period of 30 seconds (1:1 ratio), or for 30 seconds followed by a rest period of 60 seconds (a 1:2 ratio).

When starting a cardio regimen, do LISS exercise for the first six weeks or so, primarily to build up your muscle, tendon, and joint strength as well as your endurance in anticipation of incorporating HIIT into your routine. Be sure to listen to your body for signs of overexertion, discomfort, or pain. It is a good idea to have your first HIIT sessions supervised in a class environment or by a qualified personal trainer. Before engaging in more demanding workouts, consult your doctor or cardiologist. HIIT is a powerful form of exercise that does not take long to do and gives you an edge on your day physically, mentally, emotionally, and, some say, spiritually!

**Resistance Training**

Resistance training makes muscles stronger and bigger, and tendons, ligaments, and bones thicker. It is also the best way for men to maintain optimal testosterone levels. Additional benefits include increased production of a brain-protecting compound, relief from stress, feelings of euphoria, more restful sleep, and greater focus.

Resistance training does not have to be complicated. After all, Conan the Barbarian built his physique just by pushing around a mill wheel! The bottom line is that there are a ton of exercises out there, and it only matters that you choose proven exercises that will not injure you over time. Be aware of what kind of exercise is enough for your level of fitness and to avoid acute injury, don't show off.

One way to break down your resistance routine is to categorize the exercises into push, pull, hinge, legs, and core. You can choose to do longer gym workouts or take shorter and more frequent "exercise snacks." Either will work. Simply follow your preference and stick to it.

Resistance exercise can be performed in many different or combined ways using weights like barbells, dumbbells and kettlebells, using your own bodyweight as in calisthenics, or using resistance bands. Whichever resistance exercise(s) you use be sure to warm-up properly and know how to perform the exercise using good form.

Upper body should be exercised 2-3 times per week and lower body should be exercised 2 times per week to gain and maintain muscle strength and mass. Try to do 20 minutes of resistance training within heart-rate zone 3 to 5 or do 5-10-minute "exercise snacks" five or six times a week. Take it slow, paying attention to your form and technique. Work up to the point where your muscles begin to feel the strain. Build up slowly, as there is no need to empty your tank completely to experience the benefits of resistance training.

Exercising the big muscles of your thighs including the glutes, hamstrings and quads, leads to an increase in the release of anabolic hormones like testosterone and growth hormone. These hormones are crucial for muscle growth and recovery and don't just act on the legs— they have systemic effects. When elevated, they promote muscle protein synthesis throughout the body, including the upper body. This hormonal boost, combined with proper nutrition and rest, can accelerate gains in upper body strength and size, so don't forget leg day!

As you get stronger and the weights you are using get easier to move around, increase your rep count to get to the point where it is difficult to maintain good form before you increase the amount of weight you use. You can also maximize your weight training by slowing down your tempo to increase the muscles time under tension. By doing so, you may enhance muscle hypertrophy (growth) and improve muscular endurance. If you are new to these concepts, it may be a good idea to use a personal trainer to guide you.

If possible, find a personal trainer to create a customized program for you that accounts for your heath history. A trainer can also teach you how to perform the exercises with good technique, ensuring your safety and success when you move on to heavier weights.

## Stretching

Lubricating the engine, checking the belts, and ensuring proper tire inflation all contribute to making sure a car continues to function well. Likewise, stretching helps to keep you in good working order. Among its numerous benefits, stretching:

- improves flexibility by increasing the range of motion in your joints. This is crucial for maintaining mobility and preventing stiffness, especially as you age.
- makes you less prone to injury.
- helps to alleviate muscle soreness and stiffness following intense exercise or physical exertion.
- can help alleviate mental stress and promote a sense of calmness and well-being.
- leads to greater efficiency of movement, which can enhance athletic performance in various sports and physical activities.
- helps to alleviate chronic pain conditions such as low back pain and muscle tension headaches by reducing muscular tightness.

In addition to improving poor posture, regular stretching can help to correct imbalances in muscle length. Overall, improved flexibility and mobility gained from stretching translate into better performance of daily activities, such as bending, lifting, and reaching, making everyday motions easier and more comfortable. Incorporating stretching into your daily routine, whether through dedicated stretching sessions, yoga, or other flexibility exercises, is essential for maintaining overall health, optimizing physical performance, and preventing injury.

Stretching is a heart-rate zone 1 activity and is best performed after exercise, when blood is in your muscles, otherwise you may be stretching ligaments or joint capsules instead of muscle. For an effective stretch, use breathing and focused calm to help relax your muscles, and make sure to be well hydrated before stretching.

There are many different types and disciplines of stretching, and all are effective when the following precepts are followed:

- Avoid bouncing.
- Breathe deeply and slowly to help relax your muscles and allow them to lengthen.
- Stretch to the point of mild discomfort, not pain, as overstretching can lead to injury.
- Slowly and patiently increase your range of motion, or how far you can go, and remember to use good form.

Compound stretching is a time saver and a great way to stretch and lubricate your body. The following compound stretches, listed by area of the body, may be especially beneficial.

### *Spine*

To stretch your spine, do a cat and camel stretch. While kneeling on all fours on the floor, make sure your hands are directly under your shoulder joints and that your knees are directly under you hip joints. To begin, arch your back and extend your neck like a cat. Then, round your back and bring your chin to your chest. (See Figure 2.2. Cat and Camel Stretch below.) There should be no pain. Gently hold each position for 5 to 10 seconds and perform three repetitions of this stretch.

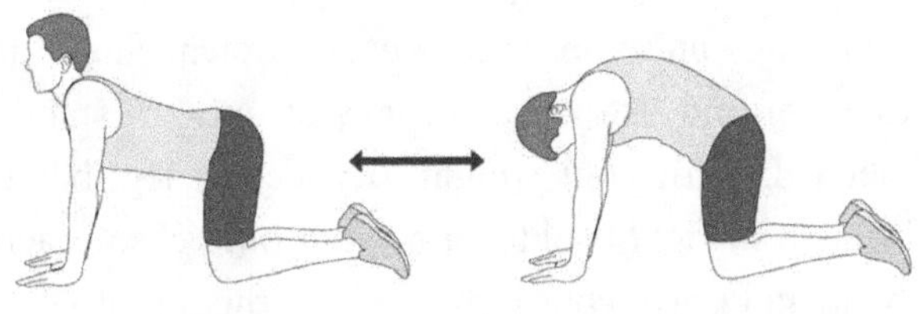

*Figure 2.2 Cat and Camel Stretch*

## *Hips, Legs, Shoulders, and Upper Back*

**To stretch your hips, legs, shoulders, and upper back, do a downward dog stretch. Start on your hands and knees** with your hands directly under your shoulders and your knees under your hips. Spread your fingers wide and press them firmly into the ground or the countertop. Tuck in your toes and lift your knees off the floor while exhaling and then extend your hips up and back. Aim to create an inverted "V" shape with your body. (See Figure 2.3. Downward Dog Stretch below.)

Maintain your head between your upper arms without letting it hang. Your ears should align with your upper arms. Hold this pose for several breaths and focus on breathing deeply and evenly. As shown in the graphic below, you may perform this stretch on the floor or using a countertop.

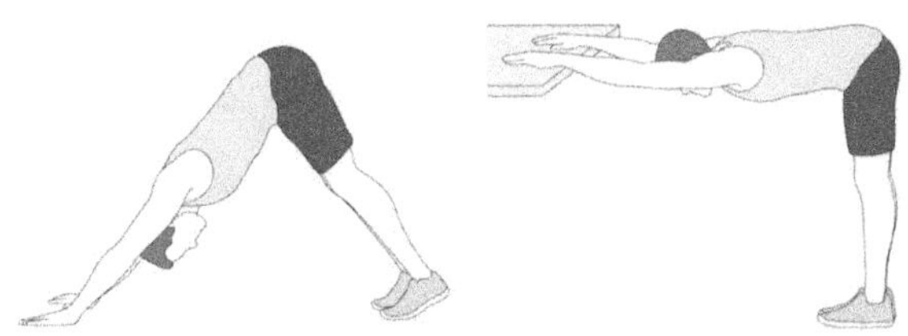

*Figure 2.3. Downward Dog Stretch*

## *Hips and Knees*

To stretch your hips and knees, do a quad stretch. Stand upright with your feet together and use a wall, chair, or another stable object for balance if needed. Shift your weight to your left leg, bend your right knee, and bring your right heel towards your buttocks. Reach back with your right hand and grasp your right ankle or the top of your right foot. Keep your knees close together and gently pull your right heel closer to your buttock until you feel a stretch along the front of your right thigh. Keep your hips aligned, avoid arching your back, and engage your core to maintain balance and proper posture. (See Figure 2.4. Quad Stretch below.) Hold the stretch for up to 30 seconds, breathing deeply and steadily. Slowly release your right foot and lower it back to the ground. Repeat the stretch on your left leg by shifting your weight to your right leg and lifting your left foot.

*2.4. Quad Stretch*

## *Hip Flexors*

We live in a "flexed" society, in which hip flexor muscles are held in a shortened position (i.e., a sitting position) and thus adapt to this shortened position and remain shortened. This reduced muscle length will lead to a pulling of the upper inner pelvis and along each side of the low-back spinal segments. If one side is tighter than the other due to sitting cross-legged on one side only, then a twisting or torquing effect is incurred on the spine and pelvis. To isolate the hip flexors when stretching, go into a lunge position and go deep into the lunge with your chest down to prevent extension of the spine and pelvis. (See Figure 2.5. Deep Lunge below.) Hold the stretch for 10 to 20 seconds and breathe deeply and steadily.

*2.5. Deep Lunge*

## *Hip Extensors and Rotators/Glutes*

Your glutes are made up of several muscles in your buttocks. Unless you work your glutes strenuously by doing an activity such as hiking, biking, weight training, or walking upstairs or hills, you may not need to stretch these muscles too much. If this muscle group could use a stretch, however, it may be stretched while you sit. Simply place the outside of one ankle on the opposite leg just above the knee and lean your chest down towards your legs. (See Figure 2.6. Sitting Stretch below.) Hold the stretch for 10 to 20 seconds and breathe deeply and steadily.

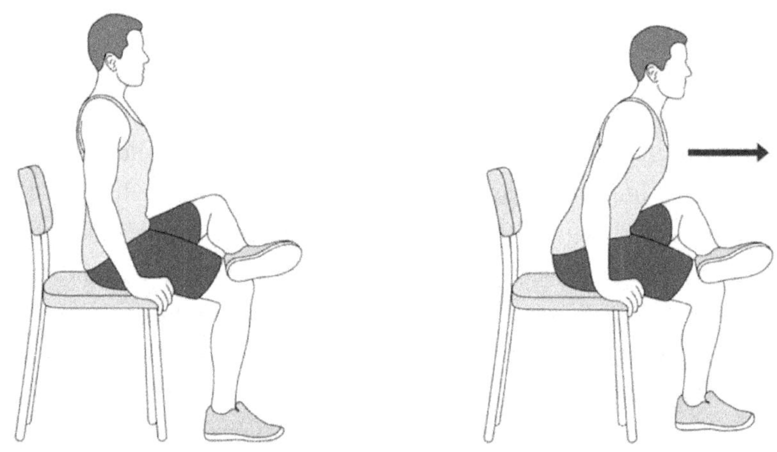

*2.6. Sitting Stretch*

## *Shoulders*

To stretch your shoulders, do a cross-body shoulder stretch, an over-head triceps stretch, and a behind-the-back shoulder stretch. To perform a cross-body shoulder stretch, stand or sit upright with your feet shoulder width apart and extend your right arm across your body at shoulder height. Use your left hand to grasp your right arm just above the elbow and gently pull your right arm across your body, keeping it straight. Hold for 10 to 20 seconds, feeling the stretch in your shoulder and upper back, and then repeat this exercise on the opposite side.

To perform an overhead triceps stretch, stand or sit upright with your feet shoulder width apart. Raise your right arm straight overhead and bend your right elbow, reaching your right hand down towards the middle of your back. Use your left hand to gently pull your right elbow closer to your head, increasing the stretch. Hold for 10 to 20 seconds, feeling the stretch in your triceps, shoulders, and upper back, and then repeat the exercise on the opposite side.

To perform a behind-the-back shoulder stretch, stand with your feet shoulder width apart and reach with both arms behind your back and clasp your fingers. Straighten your arms as much as possible while keeping your hands clasped. Lift your arms slightly away from your back, aiming to keep your elbows straight but not locked, and gently lift your chest and roll your shoulders back and down. Squeeze your shoulder blades together to deepen the stretch. (See Figure 2.7. Shoulder Stretches, Overhead Triceps Stretch, Behind-the-Back Shoulder Stretch below.) Hold for 10 to 20 seconds, breathing deeply and steadily. Slowly release your hands and bring your arms back to your sides.

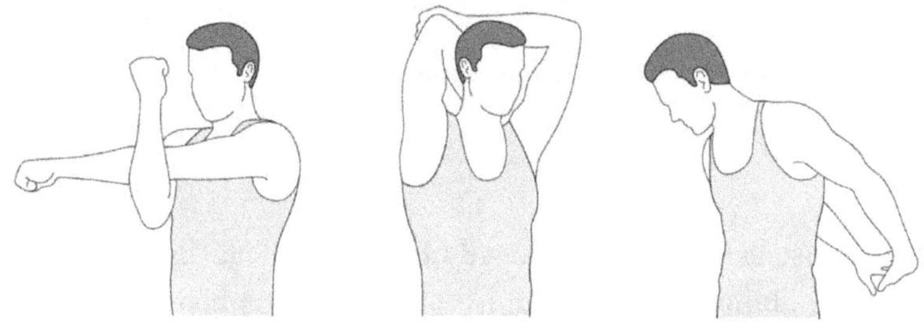

*Figure 2.7. Shoulder Stretches*

### *Forearms and Fingers*

To stretch your forearms and fingers, do a wrist flexor stretch, and a wrist extensor stretch. To perform a wrist flexor stretch, stand or sit with your back straight and your right arm extended in front of you at shoulder height, palm facing down. With your other hand, gently pull back on the fingers of the extended hand, bending the wrist upward. Hold for 10 to 20 seconds and then repeat the exercise with the opposite arm.

To perform a wrist extensor stretch, stand or sit with your back straight and your right arm extended in front of you at shoulder height, palm facing down. With your other hand, gently pull back on the hand of the extended arm, bending the wrist downward. (See Figure 2.8. Wrist Flexor Stretch and Wrist Extensor Stretch below.)

Hold for 10 to 20 seconds and then repeat the exercise with the opposite arm.

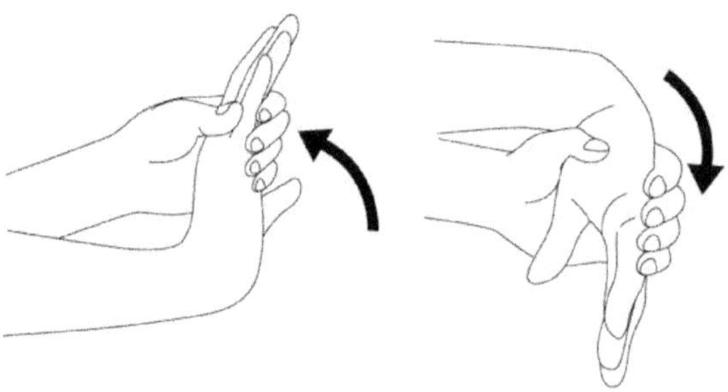

*Figure 2.8. Wrist Flexor Stretch and Wrist Extensor Stretch*

## NOTE

View exercise as a privilege instead of a punishment. Be grateful each day for the ability and opportunity to move your body, as there are people out there who'd do anything to be active. Prioritize exercise in your daily life, as it truly is the closest thing to the fountain of youth!

# Chassis—Core

"Your core muscles play a huge role in your stability and strength. When your core is strong, your whole body is stronger."

—Brett Hoebel

A well-built chassis and frame provide a car with stability and structural integrity, contributing to safer handling and performance on the road. A good chassis holds everything together just like a strong core gives you stability and allows you to maintain balance as you perform various activities, including walking, lifting, and bending. The core comprises muscles in the abdomen, back, and pelvis and connects the lower and upper body, acting as a central link that facilitates the transfer of force between these regions. This connection is crucial for maintaining stability and balance during movement, enabling efficient and coordinated actions. This functionality is essential for activities requiring power and precision, such as lifting, running, and throwing, where the coordinated movement of the entire body is necessary for optimal performance and injury prevention.

Just as a well-tuned suspension system and responsive steering in a car enhance control and handling, improving driver responsiveness and safety on the road, core strength enables dynamic control and responsiveness of human movement, allowing for quick adjustments and efficient biomechanics. This is particularly important in activities that require agility, coordination, and balance.

A strong core supports proper postural alignment by giving stability to the low back and pelvis, thereby reducing strain on muscles and joints and promoting overall comfort and well-being. Good posture, as mentioned in Part 1, is essential for maintaining a healthy spine and preventing musculoskeletal issues.

A well-engineered drivetrain and transmission system in a car ensure smooth power delivery and efficient energy transfer from the engine to the wheels, boosting performance and fuel efficiency. Likewise, a strong core allows for efficient energy transfer while optimizing movement patterns and reducing wasted energy. This is essential for activities that require power generation and endurance, such as lifting heavy objects or participating in sports.

**MAINTENANCE GUIDE**

To build up your core strength, perform the following exercises 3 to 5 times a week. Each session should take only a few minutes. The first three are known as the McGill Big 3, which are exercises that were scientifically developed by Dr. Stuart McGill of the University of Waterloo to support core stability and strength.

## Bird Dog

To perform a bird dog, first kneel on all fours on a padded floor and make sure your shoulders are directly under your shoulder ball and socket joints, and that your knees are directly under your hip ball and socket joints. Reach forward with either arm and press behind with your opposite leg, so that you fully extend your arm and leg. Hold this position with your abdominal muscles engaged. All movements are to be performed while keeping your spine in a neutral position. (See Figure 2.9. Bird Dog below.) Hold for 10 seconds and then switch sides. Perform three repetitions of this exercise. If one side is less stable than the other, start with the weaker side to help balance out the muscles of your back.

*Figure 2.9. Bird Dog*

**Side Plank**

To perform a side plank, lie on your left side with your knees bent at 90 degrees, leaning on your left elbow and hip. Make sure the elbow that is supporting you on the ground is directly under your shoulder joint and that your right hand is resting on your right hip. Now raise your left hip off the ground to achieve a neutral spine position. Try to keep your shoulders from rising to your ears and tuck in your chin a little. (See Figure 2.10. Side Plank below.) Apply the "weak side" rule, as described in the previous exercise, here as well. Hold for 10 seconds and then switch sides. Perform three repetitions of this exercise.

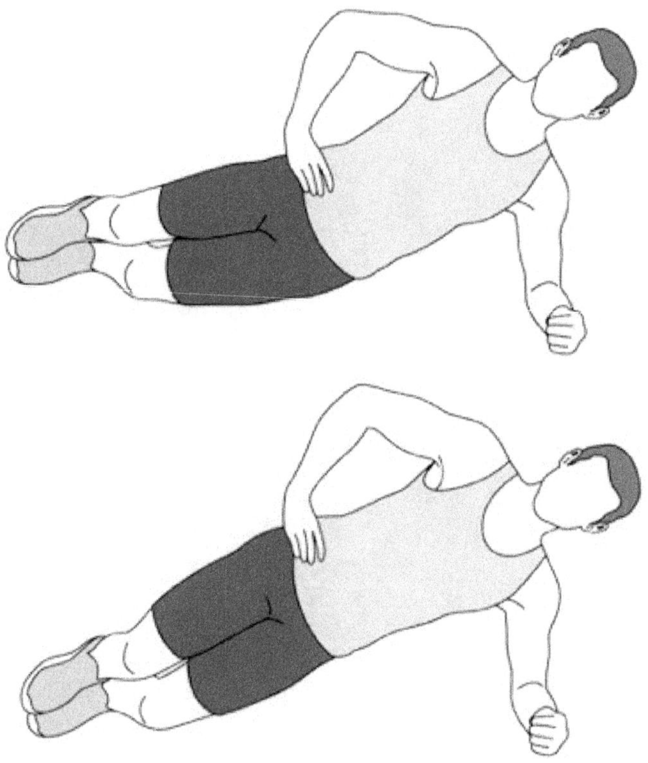

*Figure 2.10. Side Plank*

## Ab Curl

To perform an ab curl, lie on your back with your knees bent comfortably. With your fingers interlaced behind your head, pull the bottom of your breast plate towards the top of your pelvis. Maintain a neutral spine and do not flex your neck forward. (See Figure 2.11. Ab Curl below.) Hold the position with your shoulder blades barely off the floor for 10 seconds and then repeat this exercise two or more times.

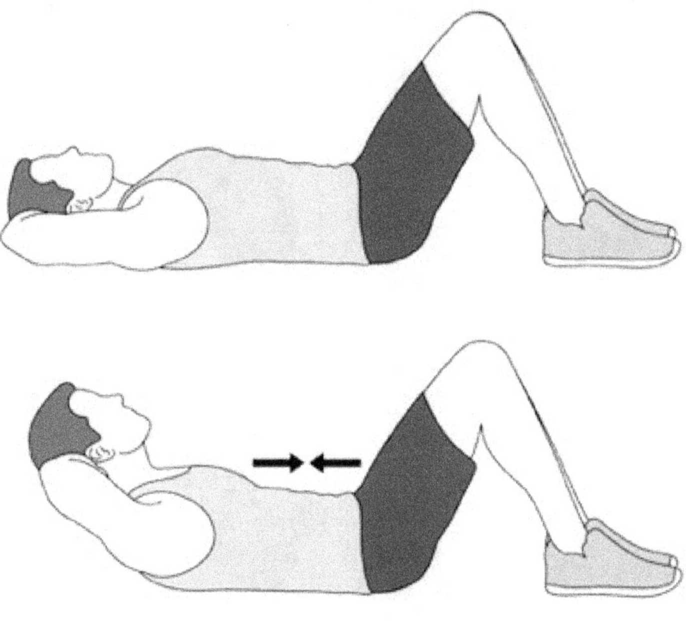

*Figure 2.11. Ab Curl*

## Glute Bridge

To perform a glute bridge, lie on your back with your knees bent and your feet flat on the floor and hip width apart. Place your arms at your sides with your palms facing down. Engage your core and glutes, and then lift your hips towards the ceiling, creating a straight line from your shoulders to your knees. (See Figure 2.12. Glue Bridge below.) Hold this position briefly, squeezing your glutes, and then slowly lower your hips back to the starting position. Start with one set of 10 repetitions.

*Figure 2.12. Glute Bridge*

## Lateral Leg Raise

To perform a lateral leg raise, also known as a "dog peeing on a fire hydrant stretch", start on your hands and knees, making sure to have a neutral spine, and use your hip joint muscles to elevate your right leg to the side while keeping your knee and hip at a 90-degree angle. (See Figure 2.13. Lateral Leg Raise below.) Do not rotate your spine to increase your range of motion but instead isolate your hip joint for the movement. As you advance, you can perform rearward circles of the leg while maintaining a bend at the knee. Start with one set of 10 repetitions each side.

*Figure 2.13. Lateral Leg Raise*

**TIPS**

To work on your core, practice engaging, bracing, or stiffening your abdominal muscles to gain control when you need it, such as when lifting objects or even just shaving in the morning. Controlled abdominal stiffening should also be employed when doing sports other activities.

# Fuel Tank—Food Quantity

"An over-eating mouth tortures the whole body."

—Amit Kalntri

A car's fuel tank has a limit for fuel intake and so do we. The problem for humans is that they possess an expandable food tank, which allows for overfilling. Eating the right quantity of food is crucial to your overall health, since the amount of food you consume plays a significant role in your maintaining a healthy weight, meeting your nutritional needs, and reducing your risks of chronic diseases. In other words, it is important to know how much to eat and when to cap your fuel tank.

Consuming an appropriate quantity of food helps your body to maintain a healthy balance between the calories you consume and the calories your body uses for energy. Generally, eating too many calories can lead to weight gain and obesity, while eating too few calories can result in muscle wasting, malnutrition, and nutritional deficiencies.

Balancing your portion sizes with your physical activity level is key to weight management. Eating the right kinds of food in the right quantities will allow you to obtain the essential nutrients your body needs for optimal health while staying trim. Consuming enough nutritious whole foods will ensure that you meet your nutritional requirements, which include vitamins, minerals, protein, carbohydrates, and healthy fats. Indulging in excessive amounts of food, especially ultra processed foods (UPFs), can overwhelm your digestive system and lead to discomfort, bloating, and indigestion. Eating appropriate portions leads to easier digestion and absorption of nutrients, promoting overall digestive health.

Eating the right quantity of food also ensures that your body has an adequate supply of energy to fuel your daily activities and maintain your vitality. Eating appropriately sized balanced meals can help you to keep your energy levels steady throughout the day and avoid energy crashes or fatigue.

## MAINTENANCE GUIDE

How much you eat really matters. As we are vulnerable to eating too much due to our expandable tank, the challenge is to recognize the satisfaction point approaching and then stop eating. Use smaller plates for your meals and stop when you feel 80-percent full. Fill up on nutrient-dense food. Chew your food thoroughly and don't eat fast. Eat at specific times and within a specific time period and try not to consume food after 8 pm at night or three hours before going to sleep.

Hydrate up to 30 minutes before eating and wait to hydrate again until at least 60 minutes after eating so as not to dilute your food and affect nutrient absorption. In addition, try completely emptying the tank at least once a week before filling up. In other words, try fasting at least once a week, as fasting may have potential health benefits, including weight loss, improved blood sugar control, heart health, enhanced brain function, and cancer prevention. We are programmed to be able to handle and benefit from fasting. Don't deprive yourself of these benefits by eating just because food is readily available.

Go for a walk after a meal, as the movement aids digestion by promoting the movement of food through the stomach and intestines, which can help to reduce bloating and discomfort. Post-meal walking also helps to regulate blood sugar and enhances insulin sensitivity, which is especially important for individuals with diabetes or insulin resistance. This light exercise also offers an opportunity to enjoy fresh air and connect with nature and can boost your overall mood.

## TIPS

It is wise to plan your mealtimes and stick to them. If you are prone to snacking too much, try to have water handy and consume it throughout the day, which should make you feel full. Be sure to exercise regularly, as exercise acts as an appetite suppressant. Finally, avoid chronic use of substances that give you the munchies (e.g., marijuana, alcohol, etc.) and steer clear of highly addictive food-like products, which have been designed to taste pleasurable but leave you wanting more.

# Fuel and Oil—Nutrients

"Unlock your full potential with nutrition."

—Every nutritionist on the planet

Car fuel and human food can be compared in several ways, particularly in terms of their impacts on the performance, efficiency, and overall well-being of a vehicle or a person. High-quality nutrients, obtained from fresh whole foods, provide the necessary energy and support for our bodily functions, much like high-quality fuel powers a vehicle efficiently.

Just as a car runs better when fueled with high-grade fuel, the human body operates optimally when nourished with nutrient-dense whole foods. Such foods contain the necessary vitamins, minerals, and energy for good health and sustained energy levels. Low-quality fuel includes contaminants that can damage a car's engine over time. It can lead to problems such as increased fuel consumption, clogged fuel filters, poor idling, stalling, fuel pump failure, engine noise, and difficulty starting. Similarly, consuming highly processed or unhealthy foods can introduce harmful substances into the body.

Regularly using low-quality fuel can lead to long-term damage to a car's engine, reducing its lifespan and reliability. In the same way, consistently consuming a diet high in unhealthy fats and sugar can contribute to long-term health problems, including heart disease, diabetes, chronic inflammation, and a reduced lifespan. In addition, manmade food contaminants like additives and conditioners can cause widespread havoc on many systems of the body.

Essential nutrients such as omega-3 fatty acids, vitamins, and minerals play a key role in countless nerve functions and cognitive processes. A balanced diet can improve mood, concentration, memory, and overall mental well-being, while reducing the risk of mental health disorders such as depression and anxiety. As omnivores, humans are designed to be able to eat a wide variety of foods. Our modern world now provides us with a large amount of low-quality but addictive food-like products. These products are tailor-made in both taste and texture for maximum addiction, but we must remember that good nutrition is vital for healthy aging and a good quality of life in later years. A diet rich in whole foods that are packed with antioxidants and other important nutrients can help to slow the aging process, preserve cognitive functioning, and reduce the risk of age-related diseases such as Alzheimer's disease and dementia. Whole foods are foods that have not been processed or made in a factory. They are usually found around the perimeter of most supermarkets and include:

- fresh meat, fish, and poultry that hasn't been preserved or processed.
- eggs, especially Grade AA pasture-raised eggs.
- vegetables.
- fresh whole fruits.
- fresh herbs.
- nuts and seeds with no added vegetable/seed oils.

## SALT

Salt, chemically known as sodium chloride, is essential for maintaining fluid balance, transmitting nerve impulses, and muscle contraction. Eating too much salt, however, can lead to health problems such as high blood pressure, stroke, heart disease, and kidney disease. If you have high blood pressure or other risk factors for cardiovascular disease, it's crucial to be vigilant about managing your salt intake. Restaurant food and processed food often contain excessive amounts of salt for flavor enhancement and preservation. Limiting the consumption of these foods can help to reduce your overall salt intake.

## CONDIMENTS

Condiments play a part in enhancing the taste of food, but they also contribute to our overall health, depending on their ingredients and level of consumption.

### Ketchup

Ketchup is high in sugar and salt, so use it in moderation.

### Mustard

Mustard is generally low in calories and does not contain unhealthy fats.

### Mayonnaise

Mayonnaise is high in calories and fat, particularly saturated fat. Choosing light or low-fat versions can help to reduce calorie and harmful fat intake.

### Soy Sauce

Soy sauce is a common condiment in many Asian cuisines. It is high in sodium, so using a light soy sauce can help to minimize your salt intake.

## Hot Sauce

Many hot sauces are low in calories, but some varieties may contain added preservatives and sugars, so remember to read labels.

## Vinegar

Vinegar can add flavor to dishes without adding extra calories or sodium. More and more studies indicate that vinegar has health benefits, such as aiding in digestion and improving blood sugar control.

## Salsa

Salsa is generally low in calories and a healthy addition to meals. When made with fresh ingredients like tomatoes, onions, and peppers, it provides vitamins and antioxidants.

## Pesto

Pesto can be high in calories and fat due to its main ingredients, which include olive oil, nuts, and cheese. Therefore, use it in moderation.

## Relish

Relish usually contains added sugars and salt, so choosing relish made with natural ingredients and no added sugar is a healthier option.

---

**Sugar**

Sugar is a simple carbohydrate commonly found in foods such as fruit, vegetables, and processed products. It can be naturally occurring or added to foods, and excessive consumption of sugar can lead to health issues like obesity and type 2 diabetes. Thankfully, sugar is generally not typically dense in fresh fruit. A medium-sized apple, for example, contains about 20 grams of sugar. In contrast, a chocolate bar contains about 35 grams of sugar, while a soft drink can have as much as 39 grams of sugar. In addition, fruit contains many different vitamins and lots of fiber, whereas sweets lack these healthy components. The relatively low sugar levels and high fiber content of fruit help to prevent sudden increases in blood sugar, which is important in the maintenance of good metabolic health. Of course, eating too much fruit is not necessarily healthy either. And watch out for dried fruit and fruit juices, in which sugar concentrations may be very high. Basically, too much sugar in the tank will ruin the engine!

---

## FAT

Car oil lubricates the engine to ensure smooth functioning and prevent damage. In humans, certain fats play a vital role in lubricating joints, supporting proper brain functioning, and supporting overall health. These important fats may be found easily in healthy types of oil. Just as a car's engine performance benefits from regular oil changes, so do the body's physiological functions, including hormone production and cellular integrity, benefit from a diet that includes healthy oils.

Using high-quality oil in a car can extend its lifespan and prevent premature wear and tear, while consuming high-quality oils in moderation can support an individual's good health. Healthy oils, such as extra virgin olive oil and avocado oil, contain powerful nutrients that reduce inflammation and support cardiovascular health.

Using low-quality or contaminated car oil can lead to engine problems and reduced performance. Similarly, consuming oil that is high in unhealthy fats, which include trans fats, and overconsumption of omega-6 fatty acids can contribute to inflammation and oxidative stress and increase your risk of chronic diseases such as heart disease and diabetes. Oxidative stress in humans and rust on a car are, in fact, similar, in that both involve damaging reactions with oxygen molecules that lead to deterioration over time. Oxidative stress in humans and rust on cars both cause cumulative damage over time, leading to weakened structures.

## Optimal Oils and Oil Levels

Just as cars require the right amount of oil to function optimally without causing damage or inefficiency, humans also need to consume oils in appropriate quantities. Consuming them in excess or improper ratios can lead to weight gain and adverse health effects. Finding the right balance and moderation is key to maintaining health in both cases.

Omega-3 fatty acids are known as essential fatty acids because we must get them from the diet. They can be found in nuts, seeds, eggs, oily fish, grass-fed meat, and dairy products. They support heart and brain health and help to maintain a healthy metabolism.

Omega-6 fatty acids are also essential fats, but in too high amounts they can be unhealthy. They are prevalent in food products such as potato chips, cookies, crackers, and many other food items made with corn oil or other vegetable oils. Unfortunately, the Western diet contains an overabundance of these foods. The ideal omega-3 to omega-6 ratio is anywhere from 1:1 to 1:4. The Western diet has an omega-3 to omega-6 ratio of anywhere from 1:10 to 1:50.

The biggest cause of chronic inflammation is excessive consumption of highly processed carbohydrates and oils rich in omega-6 fatty acids, such as soybean, corn, and sunflower oils, which are found in most processed foods. This chronic inflammation causes injury to blood vessels and over time paves the way for high blood pressure, type 2 diabetes, heart disease, Alzheimer's disease, weight gain, chronic fatigue, and hormonal imbalances.

**Healthy Oils**

Olive oil and avocado oil are considered healthy choices. These fats can help reduce LDL cholesterol levels (the "bad" cholesterol) while maintaining or increasing HDL cholesterol levels (the "good" cholesterol), thereby supporting heart health. Some oils, such as extra virgin olive oil, contain antioxidants and phytonutrients that provide additional health benefits. These oils may help protect cells from damage caused by free radicals and contribute to overall health and longevity.

**Unhealthy Oils**

Oils containing trans fats, hydrogenated fat, and partially hydrogenated fat are typically man-made. They are considered unhealthy and should be avoided, as they can raise LDL cholesterol levels and lower HDL cholesterol levels, increasing the risk of heart disease, stroke, and other cardiovascular problems. Unhealthy oils are often found in processed and fried foods, baked goods, and fast food. It's important to read food labels carefully and choose products that have been made with healthier oil options or prepared using healthier cooking methods.

In addition, avoid rancid oil, which could be any oil, but unsaturated oils, which include canola, olive, peanut, and vegetable, tend to go bad quickly. Overall, go easy on oil ingestion, as industrial oil creation may be contaminated with microplastics and chemicals known as phthalates, which are harmful to both physical and psychological health.

## MAINTENANCE GUIDE

Eat "high-octane," or nutrient-dense, foods. There is no best diet for everyone, but what we do know is that you need to fill up on quality protein, healthy fats, vegetables, and fruit (low-glycemic fruit, preferably). Low-glycemic foods have a moderate effect or no effect on blood glucose levels, keeping you in the healthy zone. High-glycemic foods can cause rapid spikes in blood sugar levels, leading to increased insulin production and potential energy crashes, and possibly contributing to weight gain and an elevated risk of developing type-2 diabetes and cardiovascular disease over time.

Ideally, you should strive to do the following:

- Remove unhealthy food from your home.
- Eat foods that have been processed or refined as little as possible, and which are free of artificial substances.
- Eat a variety of vegetables to ensure a broad range of nutrients.
- Read labels carefully for a product's sugar, salt, and saturated fat contents.
- Cook mostly by steaming, poaching, boiling, or roasting, if possible.
- Use stainless steel or ceramic pots and pans to avoid "forever chemicals" found in nonstick pans.
- Fry with ghee, butter, tallow, or coconut oil. Use avocado or olive oil for drizzling over salads or blending into smoothies, or as a base for dressings or marinades.

- Do not burn your food during the heating process and minimize char when barbecuing.
- Establish your relationship with food. (In other words, ask yourself why you eat?)
- Eat locally grown foods, which will be less nutritionally degraded than the alternative.
- Choose in-season foods for optimal nutritional content.
- Pack a lunch or seek out good options when eating out or getting take-out. Know what you are eating.
- Eat fat and protein before consuming sweets, which will help to reduce the rapid blood sugar spike and crash caused by eating sugar alone.
- Be aware of the oils found in the salad dressings you use at home and in the restaurants at which you eat.
- Purchase smaller bottles of oil to decrease the oxidative effects that occur from the oil sitting on the shelf for a long period of time.
- Close bottles of oil properly and avoid light exposure by keeping them in a cupboard.
- Seek single-origin oils. These oils are often of higher quality than blended oils because they require greater control over growing conditions, harvesting, and processing, which can result in a superior oil.
- Choose non-fried foods.
- Try not to overeat nuts or nut butters, as these butters provide a high amount of fat in a small serving size.

Generally, we know what is bad for you, but we don't know specifically what fuel will work best for you as an individual. Figure out what you are missing, what you are eating too much of, and what is irritating or harming your system, and then make some changes. Consider visiting a nutritionist or another qualified health professional for advice on building an individualized eating plan.

# RPMs—Metabolism

"Your metabolism is not only about how many calories you burn, but how your cells transform those calories into energy and how efficiently your body uses that energy."

—Dr. Mark Hyman

Just like a car's engine converts fuel into energy to power the vehicle, human metabolism converts food into energy to power various bodily functions. Metabolism, or metabolic rate, is like the RPMs, or revolutions per minute, of a car motor. At idle, a car's engine has a low RPM, just as your metabolism slows down to conserve energy stores when you are at rest. When a car accelerates, its RPMs increase to meet the demand for power. Similarly, when we engage in physical activity, our metabolism ramps up to supply the energy needed for movement.

Both a car's engine and the human body convert fuel into energy, but they do so in different ways. In a car engine, this process involves combustion; in a human being, it occurs through metabolic processes such as glycolysis and cellular respiration. Ultimately, efficiency in energy production is essential for optimal functioning, whether you are talking about a car or a human being.

## MAINTENANCE GUIDE

As you might have already guessed, regular maintenance is necessary for both car engines and the human engine. For a car, this might involve oil changes, filter replacements, and tune-ups. Similarly, the body requires proper care through exercise, adequate sleep, and medical check-ups in order to maintain good metabolic health.

Just as a car engine produces exhaust fumes that need to be expelled, the body produces waste products, including carbon dioxide, urea, feces and sweat, which need to be eliminated. Proper waste management is crucial for both a car and a body to function effectively.

An efficient car engine maximizes fuel economy and minimizes emissions. Similarly, a healthy metabolism utilizes nutrients optimally, maintains stable blood sugar levels, and avoids excessive fat storage. Factors that slow an individual's resting metabolic rate below a normal level include excessive body fat, as fat cells are "sluggish" and burn far fewer energy molecules (calories) than do most other tissues of the body. Furthermore, crash dieting, starving, or fasting—that is, eating too few calories—encourages the body to slow its metabolism to conserve energy.

Other metabolism killers include:

- **lack of sleep.** Inadequate sleep can disrupt hormone levels, leading to a decrease in metabolism and an increase in appetite.
- **high stress levels.** Chronic stress can elevate cortisol levels, which may lead to an increase in fat storage and a reduction in the metabolic rate.
- **sedentary lifestyle.** Lack of physical activity can slow down metabolism over time. Regular exercise helps to maintain muscle mass and is crucial for a healthy metabolism.

- **poor dietary choices.** Diets high in processed foods, sugary snacks, and unhealthy fats can negatively impact metabolism. In addition, as mentioned above, consuming too few calories can also slow down metabolism, as it encourages the body to go into conservation mode.
- **skipping meals.** Irregular eating patterns or skipping meals can cause the body to conserve energy, slowing down metabolism. It can also lead to overeating later in the day.
- **dehydration.** Not drinking enough water can impair metabolic functioning. Water is essential for various metabolic processes in the body.
- **aging.** Metabolism naturally slows down with age, primarily due to a loss of muscle mass and changes in hormone levels.
- **medical conditions and medications.** Certain medical conditions such as hypothyroidism, and medications such as antidepressants, can affect metabolism. It's important to consult with a healthcare professional if you suspect that a medical issue might be impacting your metabolism.

Ideally, you should strive to have a "clean-burning engine," which is, in part, accomplished by consuming high-quality foods that are free of additives.

# Battery—Energy

"A man doesn't need brilliance or genius; all he needs is energy."

—Albert M. Greenfield

While a car battery stores electrical energy to power various components of a vehicle, the human body stores energy in the form of calories. A car battery converts stored chemical energy into electrical energy to power the vehicle's electrical systems. Similarly, the human body converts stored energy from food (in the form of carbohydrates, fats, and proteins) into usable energy through metabolic processes like glycolysis (i.e., the conversion of carbohydrates into energy) and cellular respiration.

Just as a car battery provides electrical energy to start the engine and power the lights, air conditioning, and other systems of a vehicle, the human body utilizes energy for various functions, including movement, digestion, circulation, and brain activity. Both systems require energy to perform their respective tasks effectively. Car batteries need to be consistently recharged to maintain their functionality, either through the vehicle's alternator while running or by external charging methods. Similarly, people need to replenish their energy stores by consuming food and staying hydrated.

Like a car battery, which has a limited capacity and can run out of charge if it is not recharged, the human body also has its limits in terms of energy reserves. Overexertion, inadequate nutrition, or lack of rest can deplete energy levels and lead to fatigue, affecting a person's overall performance and well-being. Just as efficient energy use prolongs the life of a car battery, adopting habits that promote energy efficiency in the body, such as regular exercise, balanced nutrition, and adequate rest, can help conserve energy and support long-term health and vitality.

Every cell in the body has microscopic batteries, otherwise known as *mitochondria,* which when well-charged provide energy for healing and repair, along with plenty of energy to perform tasks throughout the day. Mitochondrial health plays a crucial role in overall energy production and the vitality of cells. Since the mitochondria are the power stations of the body, their health status impacts general energy levels and overall well-being. Healthy mitochondria even produce antioxidants ("rust" protection) and have mechanisms to temper oxidative damage, thereby protecting cells from the effects of oxidative stress.

Healthy mitochondria are essential for optimal muscle functioning, strength, and endurance. They are also crucial in maintaining brain health and proper cognitive functioning. Alternatively, mitochondrial dysfunction can contribute to muscle weakness, fatigue, inflammation, and impaired physical performance.

## MAINTENANCE GUIDE

When it comes to keeping your inner batteries in good working order, sleep is key. As a man, it is also important to know that a good sleep contributes to ideal levels of testosterone as well. Aim to get seven to nine hours a night. It is helpful to have a sleep routine that includes:

- avoiding screens for one hour before bed.
- making your room as dark as possible.
- setting your room temperature at about 16°C, or 61°F.
- going to bed at the same time every night.

Figure out what level of mattress firmness works best you. Generally, a firmness of 6 to 8 out of 10 works best for men. It is also helpful to take naps of 20 to 30 minutes each to catch up on sleep. Other factors that impact your restfulness include:

- **nutrition.** Focus on consistently eating nutrient-dense foods.
- **exercise.** Resistance training and activating big muscle groups can encourage proper rest.
- **behavior.** A calm demeanor leads to a good sleep.
- **spending time in nature.** Taking nature walks and breathing in clean air support a restful sleep.
- **spending time with people.** Engaging in meaningful discussions with others and sharing love and laughter is a surefire way to sleep well.
- **pets.** The unconditional love and companionship of a pet can support peaceful rest and relaxation.
- **giving blood.** Giving blood offers both psychological and physiological benefits.
- **supplementation.** Using your personal and familial history, try to identify any nutritional deficiencies you might have. In addition, consult a healthcare practitioner who knows about the subject and can determine which nutrients are low in your system and help you to address the issue through supplementation.
- **sauna therapy.** Involving exposure to high heat, sauna therapy has been shown to support mitochondrial health through several mechanisms, including the heat stress response, improved blood flow, oxygen delivery, and more.

**NOTE**

If you are going to bed pain-free but waking up in pain, you have either a bed or pillow problem or a lingering inflammatory issue. See your mechanic—I mean, your doctor—to find out.

# Fluids—Hydration

"Water is life's matter and matrix, mother and medium. There is no life without water."

—Albert Szent-Gyorgyi, MD

In both cars and humans, monitoring fluid levels regularly and ensuring they remain within appropriate ranges is essential for optimal performance and functionality. Neglecting fluid maintenance can lead to mechanical breakdowns in automobiles and humans. Therefore, whether you're talking about your car or your body, staying attentive to fluid levels and addressing any deficiencies promptly is crucial.

Water is essential for various bodily functions, including regulating body temperature, transporting nutrients, and removing waste products. Maintaining proper hydration levels is vital, as dehydration can lead to fatigue, impaired cognitive functioning, and even organ failure.

Fluid balance is necessary in regulating blood pressure, body temperature, and electrolyte levels. Electrolytes such as sodium, potassium, and chloride play major roles in nerve functioning and muscle contraction. Imbalances in electrolyte levels can disrupt these functions, leading to symptoms like muscle cramps, weakness, and irregular heartbeat.

Every system and organ, from the brain and heart to the muscles and skin, relies on adequate hydration to function optimally. Water facilitates nutrient transport, aids in digestion, cushions joints, and flushes out toxins and waste products. Therefore, adequate fluid intake is not merely a matter of quenching thirst but a prerequisite for supporting vital physiological processes and promoting overall health.

Furthermore, hydration is essential for maintaining proper cognitive functioning, as even mild dehydration can impair concentration, alertness, and memory. Additionally, adequate fluid intake promotes healthy skin by keeping it hydrated, supple, and resilient to environmental stressors. Overall, maintaining optimal fluid balance is crucial for supporting the intricate interplay of bodily systems and preserving good health.

Staying hydrated involves more than simply drinking water; it requires mindful consumption and an awareness of your hydration needs. Consuming water-rich foods like fruits, vegetables, and soups can supplement hydration while providing essential nutrients. Urine color and frequency of urination can serve as indicators of hydration status, with pale yellow urine signifying adequate hydration. Normal peeing frequency is about six to seven times per twenty-four-hour period. Try not to hold your urine in for long periods of time, as this can lead to the flourishing of bacteria in the urinary tract, which may then cause a urinary tract infection.

Additionally, incorporating hydration breaks into your daily routine and carrying a reusable water bottle can help to maintain consistent fluid intake throughout the day. By adopting these strategies, you can effectively meet your hydration needs.

Failure to remain adequately hydrated can have detrimental effects on your health and performance. Dehydration can lead to symptoms such as thirst, fatigue, dizziness, and headache. Prolonged or severe dehydration can result in electrolyte imbalances, kidney stones, urinary tract infections, and heat-related illnesses. Moreover, chronic dehydration has been associated with an increased risk of certain health conditions, including kidney disease, constipation, and urinary incontinence. Prioritizing hydration is essential for preventing these adverse outcomes and preserving optimal health.

Plain water is the best choice for quenching your thirst. Coffee or tea without added sweeteners is also a healthy choice. Other acceptable drink choices include flavor-infused water, sparkling water, and homemade smoothies. Some beverages should be limited or consumed in moderation, including fruit juice, milk, and those made with low-calorie sweeteners, such as diet drinks.

## MAINTENANCE GUIDE

You should aim to drink six to eight glasses of fluid a day. To achieve this goal, get a reusable water bottle, fill it with plain water, and take sips throughout the day. Attempt to consume clean, filtered, contaminant-free water. Furthermore, due to the possibility of microplastic infiltration, try not to drink fluids from plastic bottles.

## NOTE

The human brain has trouble distinguishing between hunger and thirst. With its intricate signals, it can occasionally blur the lines between the two sensations. So, next time you feel hunger pangs, it might be worth drinking some water before reaching for a snack.

# Visibility and Awareness—
# Vision and Hearing

"Taking care of our eyes is one of the simplest ways to take care of our future selves."

—Dr. Jeffery Anshel


"Hearing loss is not just an ear issue; it's a quality-of-life issue."

—Dr. Charles Limb


A car's windshield and headlights and a person's eyes can be compared in several ways, particularly in terms of their impacts on visibility, safety, and overall enjoyment of the ride of life. Your eyes are like a car's windshield in that they are responsible for providing a clear view of the road ahead. Over time, a windshield can get dirty, scratched, or cracked, which diminishes its clarity and makes it harder to see obstacles or read road signs. Similarly, your eyesight can deteriorate due to factors such as age, strain, or disease, making it harder to see the world around you. Regular eye exams and proper eyewear are like cleaning and repairing your windshield; they keep your vision clear and help you navigate life safely. In today's world, we have access to incredible technology coupled with skilled doctors that can help with many eye issues.

When you're driving, being aware of your surroundings is crucial for safety. In addition to maintaining good visibility, you also need to hear the sounds of other vehicles, honking horns, and emergency sirens to respond appropriately and avoid accidents. If your awareness is diminished by loud music, a malfunctioning radio, or impaired hearing, you risk missing important auditory cues that could warn you of danger.

Your hearing health plays a critical role in your ability to navigate the world safely and effectively. Good hearing allows you to pick up on subtle sounds that signal changes in your environment, such as a doorbell, a phone ringing, or someone calling your name. It also helps you engage in conversations and connect with others, much like how a driver needs to communicate with passengers and respond to external sounds. Getting regular hearing check-ups, avoiding excessive noise exposure, and using hearing aids if necessary are the same as keeping your car's audio systems in good working order and making sure your favorite tunes aren't negatively affecting your awareness on the road. They are all meant to keep you safe.

**MAINTENANCE GUIDE**

Maintaining eye health is essential, especially with the increased screen time many people experience today. The following exercises and habits can help you to keep your eyes healthy:

- Every 20 minutes, look at something 20 feet away for 20 seconds. This helps reduce digital eye strain and gives your eyes a break from focusing on screens.
- Consciously blink your eyes every few seconds for a minute. Blinking helps to moisten your eyes, reducing dryness and irritation.
- Imagine a large figure eight about 10 feet in front of you. Trace the figure eight with your eyes, slowly moving in one

direction, and then switch directions after a minute. This exercise improves the strength and flexibility of your eye muscles.

- Hold your thumb a few inches away from your face and focus on it for 15 seconds. Then shift your focus to something 10 to 20 feet away for another 15 seconds. Repeat this exercise several times. Focus shifting strengthens your eye muscles and improves your ability to focus.
- Slowly roll your eyes in a circular motion—first clockwise and then counterclockwise. Repeat this exercise a few times. Eye rolling helps to relieve tension in the eye muscles.
- Take regular breaks from screen time, at least every hour, to reduce strain on your eyes and help prevent fatigue.

Maintaining hearing health is essential especially with the noisy environments that we encounter. The following tips can prevent hearing loss and possible negative outcomes like dementia that have an increased risk with hearing loss. The following are some tips to help maintain hearing health:

- Avoid sounds above 85 decibels, such as loud music or machinery.
- Wear earplugs or earmuffs in noisy environments, like concerts or construction sites.
- Listen to music at no more than 60% volume for no more than 60 minutes at a time.
- Keep devices like TV, music players, and car stereos at a moderate volume.
- Avoid using cotton swabs or Q-tips in ears as these can push earwax further in, risking injury and infection.
- Give your ears a rest after prolonged exposure to noise.
- Early detection can help manage and prevent further hearing loss and stem dementia
- Avoid medications that can damage hearing.

## TIPS

Ensure that your workspace is well lit to reduce strain on your eyes. Position your screen about 20 to 30 inches from your eyes, looking somewhere between the middle and top of your monitor's screen.

Consume foods rich in vitamins A, C, and E, omega-3 fatty acids, and zinc, such as leafy greens, fish, eggs, and nuts, which all contribute to good eye health. Finally, stay hydrated. Drinking enough water helps to maintain moisture in your eyes.

# Grille—Teeth

"Be true to your teeth and they won't be false to you!"

—Soupy Sales


While a car's grille and a person's teeth are not quite as analogous as they seem—the grille of a car aids in the intake of air to the engine for cooling, and human teeth enable a person to bite and chew food for digestion—they nevertheless both provide protection to vital components. A car's grille shields the engine and radiator from debris, while a person's teeth protect the tongue and aid in speech. Additionally, a car's grille can enhance the appearance of the vehicle, while a person's teeth contribute to their smile and facial aesthetics. And, as you might have already suspected, regular maintenance is required for both car grilles and teeth.

Cleaning your teeth is important to prevent debris buildup and prevent decay. Moreover, dental health is critical for good overall health but is often overlooked. Beyond aesthetics, dental health plays a pivotal role in a person's well-being and quality of life. Neglecting dental care can lead to oral health issues such as cavities and gum disease. These conditions not only cause discomfort and pain but also have broader implications for general health. Research has established links between poor dental health and systemic diseases like diabetes and heart disease.

## MAINTENANCE GUIDE

The mouth serves as a gateway to the body, and its condition significantly influences overall health. To keep your teeth and mouth in good condition, remember to floss your teeth and then brush them for 2 minutes twice a day. Schedule routine dental check-ups with your dentist and eat a balanced diet that is low in sugar and rich in nutrients, which will strengthen your teeth and gums. Avoid tobacco products and consume alcohol only in moderation, if at all. Using a toothpick after meals is also a good post-meal habit to acquire. Consider using a toothpaste that does not contain chemicals that disrupt the normal bacteria culture in your mouth (i.e., read the label).

# Air Intake—Lungs

"If I had to limit my advice on healthier living to just one tip, it would be to learn how to breathe correctly."

—Andrew Weil

In a car, the air intake system is responsible for bringing air into the engine to provide it with the necessary oxygen for fuel combustion. In humans, the lungs take air into the body, allowing the oxygen it contains to be transported to cells for energy production. Both systems incorporate a filtration mechanism. In cars, the air filter removes dirt, dust, and other contaminants from incoming air, preventing them from entering the engine and causing damage. In humans, the lungs, in addition to taking in oxygen and releasing carbon dioxide, act as a filtration system, removing particulate matter and pathogens from the air we breathe and protecting their own delicate structures. (Cigarette smoke, however, has no problem bypassing the lungs' filters and damaging the lungs directly.)

Both a car's air intake system and a person's lungs are affected by the quality of air in their respective environments. Polluted air can lead to increased wear and tear on a car's air filter, potentially reducing engine performance. Similarly, exposure to air pollution can harm respiratory health, leading to conditions such as asthma, bronchitis, or other respiratory illnesses.

A clean air filter in a car ensures optimal air intake, which contributes to better engine performance and fuel efficiency. Similarly, a healthy respiratory system leads to efficient oxygen exchange, supporting physical endurance and overall well-being. And just as you can optimize a car's intake system for performance or fuel efficiency, so, too, can an individual's respiratory system be strengthened.

## MAINTENANCE GUIDE

Both types of air intake systems require regular maintenance to ensure optimal performance. In cars, the air filter needs periodic replacement or cleaning to prevent clogging, which could impair engine efficiency. Likewise, the respiratory system requires care to maintain its health. Regular exercise, whether LISS and/or HIIT, and avoidance of harmful pollutants help to keep the lungs functioning properly. In addition, breathing techniques such as deep breathing or diaphragmatic breathing can optimize oxygen intake in humans, improving overall respiratory efficiency and oxygenation of tissues.

As a breathing exercise, inhale deeply through your nose and feel your ribcage expand in all directions. Once fully inflated, hold your breath momentarily, fully exhale, feel your ribcage contract and fold in completely, hold momentarily, and repeat.

Practice these full inhalations and exhalations a few times a day to maintain the strength of the muscles of the respiratory system, including the diaphragm and the intercostal muscles (i.e., the muscles between your ribs). Ribs are supposed to move up and down like a bucket handle and settle in a neutral position (somewhere between bucket handle up and down) when at rest.

Maintaining a neutral posture helps to keep the ribs in an ideal position and allows for a balanced musculature. If necessary, see a chiropractor to help deal with rib mobility issues, which includes a lack of movement due to chronic poor posture that creates shortened chest muscles and weak upper back muscles.

Last but certainly not least: Don't smoke.

**CAUTION**

If you get something stuck in your air intake, like a piece of steak or a bone, and have difficulty breathing, do not isolate yourself and try to free what is causing the obstruction on your own, as you may need help. It is important to make sure that someone knows you are choking, as it could be a life-threatening situation. In addition, be sure to learn how to perform the Heimlich maneuver, a first-aid method designed to dislodge an obstruction in the airway. You can perform this potentially life-saving technique on yourself if necessary, or on a loved one who is choking.

# Exhaust—The Lower Digestive and Urinary Tracts

"You are what you eat, so don't be cheap, easy, fast, or fake."

—Tehzeeb Lalani

Both a car's exhaust system and a human's digestive and urinary systems are responsible for removing waste. A car's exhaust fumes are expelled through the exhaust pipe after being filtered by the catalytic converter. The exhaust system ensures that gases are directed away from the engine and the car's interior to prevent buildup and maintain safety. Similarly, the human body expels liquid waste (i.e., urine) through the urinary system and solid waste (i.e., feces) through the digestive system (as well as removing carbon dioxide through the respiratory system, as previously discussed.)

A car's exhaust system includes components such as the exhaust manifold, catalytic converter, muffler, and tailpipe, while the lower gastrointestinal, or GI, tract comprises organs such as the large intestine, colon, rectum, and anus.

Anal health is often overlooked but crucial for maintaining comfort and preventing certain health issues. The anal area plays a crucial role in the digestive process, as it is the endpoint of the digestive tract—the place where waste products are expelled from the body. Keeping the anal area clean and healthy supports proper bowel movements and digestive functioning. Maintaining anal health can also help you to avoid common anal conditions such as hemorrhoids, anal fissures, and anal itching. These conditions can be painful and uncomfortable and may require medical treatment if left untreated.

Paying attention to anal health can help to detect potential health issues early on as well. Symptoms such as bleeding, pain, or changes in bowel habits may indicate underlying conditions such as inflammatory bowel disease (IBD) or colorectal cancer. Seeking prompt medical attention for any concerning symptoms is essential for prompt diagnosis and treatment.

Your urinary system is made up of your kidneys, ureters, bladder, and urethra. It prevents waste and toxin buildup in your blood and controls the levels of chemicals and salts in your blood. It also helps to maintain your body's water balance. Common urinary tract problems include urinary tract infection (UTI) and kidney stones. There are many more, so be sure to consult your healthcare professional if you have symptoms such as painful urination, difficulty urinating, or a dramatic increase in urination frequency.

**Urinary tract infections** are often caused by bacteria entering the urinary tract. Symptoms include a strong and persistent urge to urinate, a burning sensation during urination, cloudy or strong-smelling urine, pelvic pain, and fever or chills. Kidney stones are hard mineral and salt deposits that form in the kidneys, with symptoms including severe pain in the side and back, pain that radiates to the lower abdomen and groin, fluctuating intensity of pain, nausea, vomiting, frequent urination, cloudy or foul-smelling urine, and pink, red, or brown urine.

Issues regarding anal and urinary health can be embarrassing, give you anxiety, and decrease your self-esteem. Open communication with your healthcare providers and seeking appropriate treatment when needed can alleviate the stress associated with these concerns.

## MAINTENANCE GUIDE

Both a car's exhaust system and a person's GI tract and urinary system require regular maintenance to ensure optimal performance and prevent problems. For cars, maintenance may involve periodic inspections, repairs, and emissions testing to ensure compliance with environmental regulations. Supporting a healthy lower GI tract and urinary system involves consuming a balanced diet, staying hydrated, and seeking medical attention for any digestive issues or concerns.

Proper anal hygiene helps to prevent infections and discomfort. Regular cleansing of the anal area, especially after bowel movements, reduces the risk of bacterial or fungal infections, as well as irritation and itching caused by fecal residue. Keep the anal area clean by washing with water every day. Don't use soap, as it will reduce the natural oils that protect the anus and may make the area dry and itchy. Use aqueous cream or a soap-free cleanser instead if you feel the need to do so.

Follow good toilet practices. Avoid vigorous wiping with toilet paper, as this may cause further chafing of the skin, which can become inflamed or infected. Avoid the use of cleansing wipes as well. Don't delay going to the toilet. If you feel the urge to go, then go. Try not to strain when going to the toilet, as this can irritate the anal area and lead to complications such as hemorrhoids.

Sit on the toilet properly. Keep your back straight, lean forward, rest your forearms on your knees, keep your knees higher than your hips by lifting your heels or using a footstool, and keep your legs apart. Finally, don't sit on the toilet for too long!

Maintaining urinary system health involves staying well hydrated by drinking plenty of water to flush out toxins and bacteria, getting regular physical activity, and having a healthy diet, all of which can reduce the risk of urinary tract infection (UTI) and kidney stones.

Avoid holding urine for extended periods and urinate after sexual activity to flush out potential bacteria. Getting regular medical check-ups and promptly addressing any urinary symptoms, such as pain or changes in urination, can also help to maintain urinary system health.

**NOTE**

If you are experiencing severe pain anywhere in your lower GI tract or urinary tract that does not improve in a few days, have been bleeding from your anus, or have noticed any new or unusual lumps in this area, it is important that you seek medical advice.

# Spark Plugs—The Reproductive System

"Reproduction is more pleasurable than death."

—Herman E. Daly

Although there is nothing quite like a reproductive system in a car, you could say that the spark plugs are the most comparable parts. Spark plugs are responsible for making the sparks that ignite the mixture of air and fuel in a car's engine, powering the pistons and thus making the car go. The male reproductive system also provides a spark: the figurative spark required for the creation of human life. The main components of the male reproductive system are the penis, testicles, scrotum, prostate gland, vas deferens, and urethra.

The prostate gland plays a key role in male reproductive health by producing seminal fluid that nourishes and transports the sperm, which is manufactured in the testicles and transported through the vas deferens tubes and out through the penis via the urethra. Prostate health is important for maintaining not only sexual health but also a healthy urinary tract. In addition, hormonal balance is essential for male reproductive health. Testosterone, the primary male sex hormone, is produced in the testicles and regulates various aspects of reproductive functioning, including sperm production, libido, and muscle mass. Imbalances in testosterone levels can affect fertility, sexual functioning, and overall health.

A man's reproductive health impacts his ability to help conceive a child. Moreover, it is also vital for the well-being of his potential offspring as well as his own overall welfare. Sperm production, quality, and motility are essential factors in male fertility, and maintaining good reproductive health increases the likelihood of successful conception and pregnancy. Male reproductive health influences sexual functions, including erections, libido (sex drive), and ejaculation. Issues such as erectile dysfunction, premature ejaculation, or low libido can affect sexual satisfaction and intimacy in relationships. Addressing these concerns can improve overall sexual health.

Reproductive health can also impact a man's mental and emotional health. Understandably, infertility or sexual dysfunction may lead to stress, anxiety, depression, or relationship difficulties. Addressing reproductive health concerns can improve mental health and overall quality of life. Male reproductive health screenings and exams can help detect and prevent various reproductive health issues, including testicular cancer, prostate cancer, sexually transmitted infections (STIs), and hormonal imbalances. Early detection and treatment of these conditions are crucial for optimal outcomes in these matters.

## MAINTENANCE GUIDE

Certain lifestyle factors, such as diet, exercise, smoking, alcohol consumption, and drug use can influence male reproductive health. Adopting a healthy lifestyle, which includes eating a balanced diet, exercising regularly, and avoiding harmful substances, can positively impact fertility, proper sexual functioning, and overall reproductive health.

To improve performance in the bedroom as well as bladder control, perform pelvic-floor exercises, which include the anal elevator, and the pee stop-and-go. The anal elevator exercise involves contracting and lifting the muscles around the anus and pelvic floor to strengthen them and improve bladder and bowel control. The pee stop-and-go involves repeatedly starting and stopping the flow of urine midstream to strengthen the pelvic-floor muscles.

To maintain your prostate health, see your doctor for regularly scheduled digital rectal exam (DRE) and prostate specific antigen (PSA) screenings, which can help to detect prostate enlargement and even cancer. Your doctor will also examine your testicles at your regular check-ups, although a possible cancerous testicular growth may also be discovered during self-examination or through examination by your partner. Doctors recommend monthly self-examination to feel for any changes in the testicles.

To perform self-examination, start on one side of the scrotum (the skin sac containing the testicles) and gently roll the scrotum with your fingers to feel the surface of the testicle. Check for any lumps, bumps, or unusual features. Make note of any changes in testicle size over time and whether there are any painful spots. Typically, cancerous tumors are not painful.

For men interested in fatherhood, maintaining good reproductive health is essential for achieving their reproductive goals and ensuring the health of their future children. Taking proactive steps to address reproductive health concerns can support family planning and parenting aspirations.

Men need to prevent unintended pregnancies, whether within or outside of marriage. They need to protect themselves and their partners against acquiring STIs, including human immunodeficiency virus (HIV), and they need to be screened and, if necessary, treated for such diseases. Furthermore, men need to be able to father children when they and their partners choose to have them, overcome fertility problems, and help ensure that their partners' pregnancies are healthy ones.

If you are sexually active, you should consult with your healthcare provider to discuss which contraceptive method would be best for you and your partner. This choice may be influenced by your or your partner's health, your or your partner's age, the frequency of your sexual activity, your number of partners, your desire to have children in the future, and your family history of certain diseases. Always use contraception carefully, consistently, and correctly.

It is important to discuss the risk factors for STIs with a healthcare provider and ask about getting tested. It is possible to have an STI and not know it, as many STIs do not cause symptoms. If you have an STI, your healthcare provider will tell you about treatment options and how to decrease or eliminate the risk of your transmitting the STI to your partner.

If you and your partner are interested in having children but having difficulty conceiving, it is important for both the male and the female partner to consult a healthcare provider to assess fertility. Over one-third of infertility cases are caused by male reproductive issues, alone or in combination with female reproductive issues. Treatments, however, are available to address many of the causes of male infertility.

# Part Three
# Maintaining Your "Vehicle"

# Pollution Control

"The impact of pollution on men's health is largely overlooked, yet research shows it plays a significant role in rising rates of cancer, heart disease, and respiratory illness. Reducing pollution is an investment in healthier lives."

— *Dr. Thomas Sanderson*

When we talk about controlling pollution for a car, we mean reducing its release of harmful emissions, which is achieved through technologies like the catalytic converter and regular maintenance to ensure the engine runs efficiently. When we talk about controlling pollution for a human, however, we mean minimizing a person's exposure to harmful stimuli. Specifically, mitigating air, light, noise, and digital pollution is crucial for maintaining good health in a human being.

## Air Pollution

Keep track of local air quality reports and pollution levels. Many governments and environmental agencies provide real-time data on air quality through websites, apps, or news channels. Avoid outdoor activities during times of high pollution if possible. Pollution levels are often higher during rush hour and in areas with heavy traffic. Try to schedule outdoor activities during times when pollution levels are lower, such as early morning or late evening.

Depending on your location, consider buying a few indoor air purifiers with HEPA filters to remove pollutants from indoor air. Place the purifiers in commonly used rooms, especially bedrooms, to ensure cleaner air while sleeping. In addition, use your exhaust fan while cooking to reduce indoor air pollution that results from cooking fumes. You should also open windows and doors when outdoor air quality is good to allow fresh air to circulate indoors. Certain indoor plants can also help to improve indoor air quality by absorbing pollutants.

**Noise Pollution**

Reducing noise pollution is essential for mental health and good cognitive functioning. Persistent noise can lead to stress, anxiety, and hearing loss. Use soundproofing measures such as carpets, heavy curtains, and insulated windows to reduce noise, and wear ear protection when necessary. You may also try to use a white noise machine to filter out disruptive noise.

**Light Pollution**

Excessive exposure to artificial light, particularly blue light from screens and unshielded outdoor lighting, can disrupt your internal clock, which is naturally aligned with the cycle of day and night. This internal clock is running in the background to carry out essential functions and processes at certain times of the cycle. Disruption of this cycle can potentially lead to sleep disorders and associated health issues such as depression and obesity. Limit screen time before bed, and if you can't, use blue light filters on your devices. Finally, ensure your sleeping environment is dark by using blackout curtains.

## Digital Pollution

Mitigating excessive use of digital devices that lead to frequent dopamine release is essential for maintaining a healthy balance in life and reducing the risk of addiction to these devices. Dopamine is a brain chemical that plays a role in how we feel pleasure and reward. Too much or too little dopamine can lead to many different health issues. The repeated stimulation of the brain's reward system can result in the development of addiction, as the brain becomes dependent on the source of stimulation, often a drug, to achieve dopamine release and associated feelings of euphoria.

Some strategies to deal with digital overexposure include:

- setting specific time limits for digital activities such as social media, gaming, and browsing the Internet. Use features like screen time controls or app timers to enforce these limits.
- avoiding mindless scrolling or constant checking of notifications by consciously choosing when and how you use digital devices.
- scheduling regular breaks from digital devices throughout the day to give your brain a rest and prevent overstimulation. Use breaks to engage in nondigital activities such as exercise, hobbies, or spending time with loved ones.
- cultivating hobbies, interests, and social connections that do not rely on digital technology. Take the time get outdoors and pursue creative activities.
- minimizing distractions and interruptions by disabling nonessential notifications on your devices.
- taking longer breaks from digital devices by unplugging for a designated period of time of more than a day, such as a weekend or vacation.
- designating specific areas in your home as tech-free zones, in which digital devices are not allowed. This can help promote relaxation, focus, and face-to-face interaction without the constant presence of screens.

- being intentional about how you use digital technology and prioritize activities that align with your values and goals. Use technology as a tool for productivity, learning, and connection, rather than as a source of constant entertainment or distraction.

If you struggle to manage your use of digital devices or feel you may be experiencing symptoms of addiction in relation to these gadgets, seek professional help. By implementing the strategies outlined above, you can reduce your exposure to digital pollution, manage your body's release of dopamine, and cultivate a more balanced and mindful relationship with technology.

# Computer—Brain

"Happiness depends more upon the internal frame of a person's own mind, than on the externals of the world."

—George Washington

While it may seem abstract, there are indeed some interesting similarities and comparisons between a car's computer and a person's psychological health. A car's computer has an operating system (OS) that controls its functions and processes data. Similarly, the human brain can be seen as the operating system for psychological health, controlling thoughts, emotions, and behavior.

Your psychological state has a dramatic effect on your body. Psychological problems have been correlated with heart related problems, decreased healing ability, and depressed immune functioning, along with compromised posture, which can cause pain.

The components of psychological health are dynamic and require appropriate attention to adjust and reset. Mental health means finding just the right balance between a lack of awareness (being oblivious) and over-attention (being constantly anxious). Either one of these positions is going to mean some kind of bad news. If you are not at ease with your own mind, it might be wise to seek professional help. There's no shame in having a skilled "mind mechanic" help you out.

## SELF-ESTEEM

The fastest route to confidence is to live your values and grow your goals. This means working gradually to self-actualize and make meaningful accomplishments. It also means being light-hearted with yourself and working towards reducing any unhelpful self-talk.

## DECISION-MAKING

Make decisions with integrity and gathered knowledge. You will not always make the right decision. If you don't make decisions, then others will for you. Let your decisions be good decisions, but if you make mistakes, acknowledge them and take responsibility. You can only make decisions with the information you have on hand. Avoid unhelpful regrets.

## COMMUNICATION

A car makes signals with its lights, but a human being makes them most effectively through language. With words, you tell others what you are thinking, what you are feeling, and what you plan to do. In general, the better you can communicate, the more satisfying your relationships with others will be. This is especially true if you are part of a family or in a significant romantic relationship. In these situations, a kind of teamwork is essential for health and happiness, and teamwork requires good communication.

## EMBRACING POSITIVE EMOTIONS

Love is something you cultivate; it takes work. You love those to whom you give. Peace and calm come from knowing what you can control, and what you cannot control. Whenever necessary, practice acceptance. Remember who has helped you. Practice a daily moment in time of remembering the good in your life. Being kind makes you happy, and others happy. Remember the Golden Rule. Feed your joy and let yourself feel your enthusiasm.

## DEALING WITH NEGATIVE EMOTIONS

According to Socrates, envy is the ulcer of the soul. And as Theodore Roosevelt once said, comparison is the thief of joy. If you often feel envious or jealous of others, remember that you must also desire the suffering they experience. Everyone experiences suffering.

In terms of anger, you may attend appropriately to legitimate threats, but you should also learn to control your anger. Uncontrolled anger will ruin your life. As Benjamin Franklin once said, whatever is begun in anger, ends in shame. You should also try to control your reactive mind. In the words of Winston Churchill, you will never reach your destination if you stop and throw stones at every dog that barks.

Give up being right all the time. Be kind. Work to create connections, both large and small. Loneliness will then diminish. Don't be afraid of what other people say or think. Be courageous by acknowledging fear and then acting. Control your fear and anxiety by thinking and acting as if you have no limits to your abilities.

If you find you have a sense of possessiveness in relation to your partner, deal with it appropriately by looking within and expanding on your own sense of identity. Pick up a hobby or do some socializing apart from your partner. Live your own life and suffer less from the pain of possessiveness.

## MAINTENANCE GUIDE

We all have the power of choice in life. We can resist what we don't like in the hope that it will go away, or we can accept things the way they are and make space for something new and different to transpire simply by being in the flow of who we are and what is happening around us. When we surrender to what is, we allow the true beauty of life to unfold. This magical space is where joy lives, and where gratitude can be found.

A few specific ways to maintain your mental health include the following:

- Be mindful and observe yourself. Scan for possible compulsive behaviors (things you do repeatedly even though they're creating negative effects).
- Be honest with yourself. Ask if your interactions leave you feeling good or bad.
- Limit your indulgence in escapist activities, as they can corrode motivation and stop you from being responsible.
- Master self-discipline and live with integrity to yourself and your values.
- Build healthy new habits. Try meditation, yoga, or tai chi, as they have been shown to help with stress, depression, and anxiety, especially in men.
- Have something to look forward to.
- Stay connected by maintaining and developing relationships with family and friends.
- Have a social network and surround yourself with like-minded people.
- Stay connected to other men, as men need a "band of brothers" for support, camaraderie, and stress reduction. A group of good friends can also keep you from getting stuck in your biases.
- If you are feeling lonely, close your eyes and visualize being surrounded by loved ones.
- Find a positive mentor or role model to emulate.
- Become a role model or mentor to someone you believe in and want to help.
- Get involved with and support a charity.
- Learn how to cope with stress through breathing and meditation.
- Get a pet. They're wonderful for companionship and unconditional love.
- Build muscle, as it protects against dementia and stroke.

If you are struggling and can't balance your negative emotions with positive emotions, consider seeking professional help. Try not to nurture a sense of victimhood, but avoid adopting a machismo mentality (i.e., an exaggerated emphasis on displaying masculinity coupled with an overly simplistic definition of what masculinity is) at all costs. It always leads to bad results.

## CAUTION

Pornography can negatively distort a man's perception of healthy relationships and intimacy. It is like malware to a car's computer. It often promotes unrealistic expectations about sex, leading to dissatisfaction with real-life partners. Over time, frequent consumption may desensitize the brain's reward system, potentially causing addiction, reduced emotional connection, and issues with sexual performance. Furthermore, it can also contribute to feelings of shame, isolation, and damaged self-esteem, adversely affecting mental and emotional well-being.

# Car Wash—Grooming

"Health is not just physical; it's emotional and mental. Grooming is part of self-care, and it tells others you respect yourself."

– Jim Kwik

Just like washing and cleaning a car maintains its look and prevents damage occurring from dirt, washing and grooming yourself removes impurities, enhances your appearance, and promotes a clean, fresh feeling. Basic grooming, such as daily cleansing, shaving, and trimming nails and hair, helps to maintain healthy skin and hair, and affects the degree to which others may be attracted to you.

Both a clean car and a well-groomed man can make a strong first impression. Whether it's in connection with a job interview or a date, your grooming and appearance convey a sense of pride and care in presentation, just as a shiny, spotless car reflects upon its owner.

**MAINTENANCE GUIDE**

A basic men's grooming routine typically includes daily cleansing of the face with a gentle face wash to remove dirt and excess oil, followed by moisturizing to keep skin hydrated, if desired. Shaving or beard trimming should be done regularly, depending on personal preference, using a clean razor or trimmer. Regular hair washing and conditioning with quality products will help you to maintain a healthy head of hair. Nail care, including trimming and cleaning, is essential, as is applying chemical-free deodorant to maintain bodily freshness for as long as possible. Periodic visits to a barber for haircuts complete the basic regimen.

## TIPS

Upon waking, move around for several minutes before going to the sink to bend over as you wash your face, and be sure to brace your core as you bend over. When shaving, you can brace yourself with your free hand as you bend over the sink if you wish. If you are shaving your head, be sure not to bend at the neck too much in an attempt to access the parts of your skull that are difficult to reach, as doing so might lead to a neck injury.

# Security System—Immune System

"Your immune system is your best friend. It protects you. It helps you heal. It's working tirelessly, even when you sleep. Treat it with respect, fuel it well, and it will take care of you."

*— Dr. Jillian Teta*

The security system of a car and a person's immune system both serve as vigilant guardians, using detection and response mechanisms to protect against external threats. A car's security system is designed to protect the vehicle from external dangers such as theft, unauthorized access, or vandalism. Similarly, the human immune system protects the body from external invaders such as viruses, bacteria, and pathogens.

In a car, sensors and alarms detect when something abnormal happens, such as a break-in attempt or unauthorized access. In a human, the immune system uses specialized cells such as white blood cells to detect and recognize foreign invaders that pose a threat. When a car's security system detects a problem, it triggers an alarm or immobilizes the car to prevent theft. Likewise, when an individual's immune system detects pathogens, it initiates an immune response, attacking and neutralizing these foreign organisms.

If a car's security system is not maintained or malfunctions, it can either fail to protect the car or give false alarms. Similarly, when the immune system is weakened (due to illness or a compromised condition), it may fail to protect the body or become overactive, leading to autoimmune disorders.

## MAINTENANCE GUIDE

Maintaining a healthy immune system involves adopting healthy lifestyle habits and practices—a common theme in this manual. Here are several ways to keep your immune system strong:

- Eat nutrient-rich foods along with foods that support the immune system, which include mushrooms, sweet potatoes, bell peppers, broccoli, papaya, sunflower seeds, green tea, turmeric, almonds, spinach, ginger, garlic, blueberries, kiwi, yogurt, kefir, sauerkraut, kimchi, and oily fish such as salmon, mackerel, or sardines.
- Limit your intake of sugar and processed foods, as these substances suppress the immune system and promote inflammation.
- Stay well hydrated to help carry nutrients to cells and flush out toxins.
- Get regular exercise to enhance circulation and enhance the functioning of immune cells.
- Get enough sleep, as this is the time that the body repairs and regenerates cells, including immune cells.
- Manage stress, as chronic stress can suppress the immune response and weaken the body's defense mechanisms.
- Limit your intake of alcohol and don't smoke, as both can damage and weaken the immune system.
- Practice good hygiene with regular handwashing and proper

oral hygiene to mitigate the spread of infections and reduce the burden on your immune system.
- Stay up to date with vaccinations by following recommended and proven vaccination schedules to protect yourself from preventable diseases.

Finally, try to get adequate sun exposure, as it encourages the body to produce vitamin D, which is essential for immune functioning. If you live in an area with little sunlight or have a vitamin D deficiency, consider taking a vitamin D supplement.

# Vintage Vehicle Care—Healthy Aging

"Growing up is optional, isn't it."

—Pete and Bas (seventy-something hip hop duo)

Both cars and people undergo a process of aging characterized by wear and tear, cosmetic changes, and increased risk of breakdowns. While cars tend to lose their value over time, people often gain intangible assets such as wisdom and experience. Their stories and contributions to family and society can be extremely valuable.

Keeping a car in decent shape for a long enough period of time that it becomes vintage, however, requires long-term investment and commitment, just as aging into a healthy "vintage" man does. Taking care of a car with regular maintenance can prolong its lifespan and save money on costly repairs. Similarly, investing in preventive healthcare and healthy lifestyle habits can improve your longevity and quality of life, and reduce your healthcare costs in the long run. Ultimately, healthy aging is a multifaceted process that involves various factors, including physical health, mental well-being, social connections, and lifestyle choices.

## MAINTENANCE GUIDE

One of the most important things you can do to encourage healthy aging is to maintain a positive outlook on life. In addition, cultivate resilience in the face of challenges and try to adapt to whatever changes and transitions come with aging. Adopting a sense of purpose, gratitude, and optimism can also promote healthy aging and enhance your overall quality of life.

Take proactive steps to prevent injuries and accidents in your efforts to ensure healthy aging. These steps include maintaining a safe home environment, practicing safe driving habits, decreasing risky behavior, using protective gear during physical activity, and undergoing regular vision and hearing screenings.

You can make a powerful and significant contribution to your healthy aging by assuming the following everyday habits.

### Engage in Regular Activity

Engaging in regular physical activity is essential for maintaining muscle strength, flexibility, cardiovascular health, and bone density. Exercise and good nutrition can create a musculoskeletal reserve for times when it may be needed. Exercise also helps to reduce the risk of chronic diseases such as heart disease, diabetes, and osteoporosis. Aerobic exercise and especially strength training are beneficial for physical health, mental health, stroke prevention, and longevity.

Remember to schedule postural, movement, core, balance, resistance, and aerobic training into your daily exercise routine. Emphasize buttock and shoulder strength, as these are the first areas to weaken with age. Include balance, flexibility, and functional exercises (e.g., tai chi, yoga, pilates, hiking, etc.) in your regimen. Perform a longer warm-up before engaging in sports or exercise, and don't forget to gently stretch afterwards, when the muscles are filled with blood and are more pliable.

## Eat a Balanced Diet

Focus on consuming a balanced and nutritious diet of whole foods to support your overall health and prevent age-related illnesses. The anti-inflammatory effects of this way of eating can fend off all sorts of diseases. Limiting intake of processed foods, sugary snacks, and excessive alcohol can also contribute to better health outcomes.

Exercise portion control and take supplements if necessary. Consult a professional to find out if you have any nutritional deficiencies and how to address them if you do.

## Get Routine Screenings

Routine health screenings and check-ups are important for detecting and managing age-related health issues such as high blood pressure, high cholesterol, diabetes, and prostate problems. Follow screening recommendations with your healthcare provider and stay up to date on preventive healthcare measures. Keep up to date with your health maintenance schedule.

## Get Adequate Sleep

"Vintage vehicles" need to allow more time for rest and recovery. Of course, adequate sleep is essential for cognitive functioning, mood regulation, and overall health at any age. Individuals should aim to get seven to nine hours of quality sleep per night and practice good sleep hygiene habits, such as maintaining a consistent sleep schedule, creating a comfortable sleep environment, and avoiding stimulants such as caffeine or electronics before bedtime.

## Maintain Social Connections

Maintaining strong social connections and staying engaged with friends, family, and community is important for mental and emotional well-being. Social support networks can provide companionship, emotional support, and a sense of belonging, which can help reduce the feelings of loneliness and isolation that can come with age. If you are having trouble keeping an active social life, identify a hobby or interest you enjoy and join a group dedicated to that hobby or interest so you can socialize with like-minded people. It is crucial to engage fully in life.

## Reduce Stress

Every human should practice stress-reduction techniques such as meditation, deep-breathing exercises, and any activities that require real-time focus.

## Maintain Your Brain

While strength training can benefit both your body and your mind (for example, strength training has been associated with as lower risk of dementia), it is vital to get some intellectual exercise to maintain your brain optimally.

Learn something new every day to exercise your mind and build a cognitive reserve. No matter your age, you can build new brain circuits (neuroplasticity) by learning and experiencing new activities, honing a new skill set, or forging a new career path. Listen to new and different kinds of music to stimulate and activate your brain, as novelty encourages neuroplasticity! Although your brain is not a muscle, you should still treat is as one. It needs to be activated and exercised to keep it in shape.

Finally, mental health is an integral component of healthy aging. Prioritize the previously mentioned health advice that promotes mental well-being, such as managing stress, staying socially engaged, and pursuing hobbies or other interests. Never hesitate to seek support from friends, family, or mental health professionals when needed.

---

**Addressing Wear and Tear**

Over time, both cars and the human body experience wear and tear. Addressing wear and tear in cars involves repairing or replacing worn-out parts to prevent further damage and ensure safe operation. Likewise, individuals need to address wear and tear on their bodies by managing stress, getting adequate rest, and seeking medical attention for injuries or other health concerns.

---

## PREVENTING RUST AND CORROSION

There are a handful of things you can do to prevent "rust" or "corrosion" from taking hold of your body, which include:

- stopping smoking
- reducing alcohol consumption
- taking a collagen supplement to help your body to build cartilage
- fasting intermittently, which can give your body a chance to use its energy for repair and building as opposed to digestion.
- reducing inflammation by cutting out foods with excessive sugar and carbs, such as bread, crackers, cakes, and cookies.
- losing weight if necessary.
- eating berries, especially blueberries and other dark berries, for their cognition-maintaining ability.

## MONITORING WARNING SIGNS

Both cars and human beings exhibit warning signs when something is wrong. Ignoring warning signs in cars can lead to breakdowns or accidents, while ignoring warning signs in your body can lead to serious medical conditions. Being aware of changes in your body and seeking medical attention for symptoms is crucial for maintaining good health as you age.

## TIPS

Men should be able to maintain a well-functioning body and mind well into older age. We just need to listen to our bodies and do the right things. Don't forget to warm up and hydrate before exercising to prevent injury, normalize your weight, and utilize a trusted professional for supplement guidance, if needed. Join a book club, cooking class, photography class, or some other group that interests you. In addition, remain aware of your personal and family health histories, which will help you to act accordingly in relation to your physical and mental health.

Moreover, if you are not already, be young in your mind and young at heart.

## CAUTION

Like most men, you have probably put off going to a mechanic after hearing a strange sound coming from your car while driving with little consequence. When it comes to your health, however, you should deal with warning signs immediately, no matter how subtle they are. Do not delay and do not wait until they get worse! Prevention and early intervention are easier and less costly than dealing with a full-blown illness.

# Vehicle History—Health History

Just as a car's history reveals its past maintenance schedule, accidents, and potential future issues, an individual's health history provides essential information on genetic predispositions, previous medical conditions, and risk factors, enabling more informed and proactive health management. A car with up-to-date maintenance records and a history of regular service is akin to a person with a solid understanding of their health status.

**PERSONAL HEALTH HISTORY**

It is recommended to create a file for your personal health history containing information regarding:

- Medications taken (past and present)
- Immunizations
- Illnesses
- Past injuries
- Surgeries
- Tests and Imaging results

Maintaining a personal health history file is crucial for managing your health and paving the way for effective medical care. A health history file also helps you track patterns or changes in your health which facilitates early detection and treatment of present and potential future health issues. Furthermore, continuity of care is made easier when transitioning between doctors and specialists, along with reducing the risk of errors.

## FAMILY HEALTH HISTORY

Having knowledge of your family health history is valuable for understanding and managing health risks and is key to proactive health care. Family health history provides insight into genetic predispositions and the likelihood of inheriting certain medical conditions. By knowing your family's health patterns, you can take preventive measures, adopt healthier lifestyle habits, and engage in early screenings and interventions. This awareness aids healthcare providers in developing personalized care plans and empowers individuals to be vigilant about their health risks.

Furthermore, discussing and documenting health history fosters communication within families, encouraging a collective approach to health and well-being. Keeping this information organized not only empowers you to take proactive steps but also supports your future generations in understanding their inherited health risks. Ultimately, this information is a foundational step in achieving better health outcomes and longevity for you and your family.

# Basic Maintenance Schedule

Basic car maintenance, like maintaining your health, ensures reliability, longevity, and peak performance, highlighting the importance of regular care and attention in all aspects of life. Regular physicals act like comprehensive inspections, catching minor issues before they escalate into costly problems. Meanwhile, milestone tests—like colonoscopies or timing belt replacements—are necessary at specific intervals to avoid major failures. While consistent care ensures longevity and efficiency, neglecting maintenance can lead to serious consequences.

Following a basic medical check-up schedule for men at different ages can help ensure you receive appropriate preventive care and screenings throughout your life. The table below (Table 3.1. Basic Maintenance Schedule) comprises general guidelines and recommendations. You may require additional testing, maintenance, or treatment based on your health history or risk factors, or as your trusted healthcare professional sees fit.

Additional tests may include a hormone panel or tests for nutrient deficiencies. Typically, a hormonal deficiency will be related to testosterone or thyroid hormones. A nutrient deficiency is often associated with having a low level of iodine, zinc, magnesium, potassium, calcium, selenium, folate, vitamin D, vitamin C, vitamin $B_6$, vitamin $B_{12}$, or vitamin A.

| 18–29 YEARS | 30–39 YEARS | 40–49 YEARS | 50–64 YEARS | 65+ YEARS |
|---|---|---|---|---|
| **Annual Checkup:** | **Checkup Every 2–3 Years:** | **Annual Checkup:** | **Annual Checkup:** | **Annual Checkup:** |
| General Physical | General Physical | General Physical | General Physical | General Physical |
| Blood Pressure | Blood Pressure | Blood Pressure | Blood Pressure | Blood Pressure |
| Cholesterol Screening | Cholesterol Screening | Cholesterol Screening | Cholesterol Screening | Cholesterol Screening |
| Discussion Of Lifestyle Habits (Diet, Exercise, Substance Use) | Diabetes screening (If risk factors present) | Diabetes screening (If risk factors present) | Diabetes screening (If risk factors present) | Diabetes screening (If risk factors present) |
| Vaccinations Review/Update | **EVERY 5 YEARS:** | **EVERY 1–2 YEARS:** | **EVERY 1–2 YEARS:** | **EVERY 1–2 YEARS:** |
| Testicular Cancer Screening: Monthly self examination | Colonoscopy Or Alternative Colorectal Cancer Screening | PSA And DRE For Prostate Cancer Screening | PSA And DRE For Prostate Cancer Screening | PSA And DRE For Prostate Cancer Screening |
| | Vision Tests Hearing Tests | **EVERY 5 YEARS:** | **EVERY 5 YEARS:** | **EVERY 5 YEARS:** |
| Become Aware Of Any Changes Or Abnormalities | Testicular Cancer Screening (Monthly Self-Examination) | Colonoscopy Or Alternative Colorectal Cancer Screening | Colonoscopy Or Alternative Colorectal Cancer Screening | Colonoscopy Or Alternative Colorectal Cancer Screening |
| Skin Cancer Screening | Skin Cancer Screening | Vision Tests Hearing Tests | Vision Tests Hearing Tests | Vision Tests Hearing Tests |
| STI Screening | STI Screening | Testicular Cancer Screening (Monthly Self-Examination) | Consider Vaccination for Shingles Pneumonia and Flu | Bone Density Screening |

*Table 3.1. Basic Maintenance Schedule*

# Conclusion

As you reach the end of this health manual, it is essential to reflect on the similarities between car care and your personal health attainment and maintenance. The path to health and vitality is a lifelong commitment, just like taking care of your vehicle. Sometimes we don't stick exactly to scheduled maintenance, but we can always get back to a proper routine. By integrating the knowledge and strategies presented in this manual into your daily life, you are setting your autopilot on the road to health.

Beyond taking preventive measures to keep their cars in good shape, car enthusiasts often tweak their vehicles to improve performance, whether it's through engine modification or parts upgrade. Similarly, men can optimize their health through exercise routines, dietary adjustments, and lifestyle changes to enhance their physical performance. Each day presents an opportunity to support yourself physically, mentally, and emotionally through making good choices. Embrace these opportunities with enthusiasm and perseverance because every positive choice counts.

Don't hesitate to seek support when needed. Whether it's from healthcare professionals, fitness experts, or your social circle, having a network of support can significantly impact your success. Surround yourself with friends who encourage and inspire you to be your best self.

If an emergency arises while you are driving your vehicle, you pull over safely and let other vehicles know of your presence. The same goes for you. Know how to deal with a health emergency by taking a first-aid course. As a man, and simply as a human being, it behooves you to learn how to protect your loved ones and yourself.

Finally, treat yourself like your favorite car and have a team of "mechanics" help you in your endeavor to lead a long, functional life. Your health is one of your most valuable assets, so protect it. Learn about your "vehicle," figure out what works best for you, and go for it! In doing so, you will not only improve your quality of life but also set a positive example for those around you. Embrace this routine and enjoy the rewards of a healthier, happier you. You and your family deserve it!

# About the Author

Ron started his coaching career as a gymnastics coach. He became the youngest representative for the Ontario Gymnastics Federation at the age of 15 and went on to coach gymnastics for over a decade at the developmental, pre-competitive and competitive levels. He was chosen from his high school to attend the Ontario Athletic Leadership Camp and went on to coach his high schools' senior girls' volleyball team. Ron's passion for fitness and health, combined with his desire to help others, guided him to a career in chiropractic. Now, after three decades of practice, he has treated and helped many people of all ages achieve better musculoskeletal health including amateur, professional and Olympic athletes. Ron's keen interest in sports led him to work on the healthcare teams at many sporting events including the Pan Am Games and the Wayne Gretzky Golf Invitational Tournament. He was an anatomy lab instructor at the University of Calgary and a modality lab instructor at the Canadian Memorial Chiropractic College. He set up factory-wide exercise programs and was a fitness consultant for two Ontario ski race teams. Known for his motivational approach and commitment to sustainable health, he has contributed to numerous publications and appeared as a guest expert at IdeaCity. His insights often emphasize the importance of core strength, balance, and functional fitness as foundations for overall health and injury prevention. This is reflected in his current practice and his lifestyle, as Ron inserts fitness into his daily routine so that he can engage in his passion sports of mountain biking, skiing and windsurfing.

**Contributors**

Jay Glickman, LPCC, Arnie Deltoff, DC, Corey Negin, MScPT, Maria De Leon, D.Ch, Kelvi Bonilla, BScPT, Jessica Maiato, Yoga and Mobility Instructor, Albina Marques-Saad, BScPT, RN, Exercise Physiology, and Joel Green, Student.

**Endnotes**

*Details on references can be found on our website at **www.theowners-manual.life***